New Choices, New Families

New Choices, New Families

How Lesbians Decide about Motherhood

NANCY J. MEZEY

The Johns Hopkins University Press
Baltimore

The Johns Hopkins University Press
2715 North Charles Street
Baltimore, Maryland 21218-4363
www.press.jhu.edu

Library of Congress Cataloging-in-Publication Data

Mezey, Nancy J., 1965–
New choices, new families : how lesbians decide about
motherhood / Nancy J. Mezey.
p.   cm.
Includes bibliographical references and index.
ISBN-13: 978-0-8018-8999-8 (hardcover : alk. paper)
ISBN-13: 978-0-8018-9000-0 (pbk. : alk. paper)
ISBN-10: 0-8018-8999-5 (hardcover : alk. paper)
ISBN-10: 0-8018-9000-4 (pbk. : alk. paper)
1. Lesbian mothers. 2. Lesbians. 3. Motherhood. 4. Lesbians—
Familiy relationships. I. Title.
HQ75.53.M49 2008
306.874′308664—dc22   2007052655

A catalog record for this book is available from the
British Library.

*Special discounts are available for bulk purchases of this book. For
more information, please contact Special Sales at 410-516-6936 or
specialsales@press.jhu.edu.*

To
Mathy Mezey
My mother, mentor, and role model

Karen Diehl
My partner, soul mate, and rock

Jack and Sophie Diehl
My children, focus, and guides to what is important in life

Contents

Preface

Lesbians have been having children in record numbers in the past twenty to thirty years, starting the lesbian baby boom. The boom began with women who became mothers within heterosexual identities and then later identified as lesbians. More recently, women within their identities as lesbians have been choosing motherhood by adopting and birthing children. The lesbian baby boom has captured the interest of politicians, academics, and the general public. Over the last fifteen years, writings on lesbian mothers have burgeoned.

This book adds to that literature by addressing the basic question of how lesbians decide to become mothers or remain childfree. The book moves away from White, middle-class models and the assumption that all lesbians, as women, want to become mothers, by looking at how structures of race, class, gender, and sexuality shape lesbians' decision-making processes regarding motherhood. By doing so, the book takes a fresh look at classic sociological questions of how social structure, culture, and human agency interact to both maintain current social conditions and create social change. The book is grounded in historical and current data, as well as ethnographic accounts from lesbians of diverse racial-ethnic and class backgrounds.

This book has three main purposes. First, it challenges biological and essentialist assumptions about the decisions lesbians make about motherhood. Second, it shows how social and cultural conditions shape individual decisions and how those conditions are shaped by structures of race, class, gender, and sexuality. These structures act to privilege and disadvantage different groups in different ways, thus affecting individual decisions. Third, the book sheds light on how lesbian families form in ways similar to heterosexual families, with key exceptions due to how sexual and gender structures shape the lives of lesbians and heterosexual women. The book not only contributes to the literature on the social construction of motherhood and multiracial feminism but also forges new ground by focusing on how lesbian families, like all American families, are the outcome of the social and cultural conditions that exist in America today.

The writing of this book involved many people to whom I owe much gratitude. The work falls into two time periods: conducting the doctoral research and then turning the dissertation into a book. From the first time period, I first of all thank the women who participated in the study. Without their generous sharing of their time and experiences, I would not have been able to conduct my research. They are the heart and soul of this study and deserve many, many thanks.

Anne Ferguson, Rita Gallin, and Steve Gold helped me formulate my topic, move through my research, and write my dissertation. Marilyn Frye challenged me to think about why researchers are so preoccupied with lesbian mothers, forcing me to consider lesbians' choices to remain childfree. Lori Post gave me added incentive to finish my doctoral work. Teri Swezey offered much support throughout graduate school. Heather Dillaway and Brooke Kelly assisted me in conducting focus groups and encouraged me throughout the entire process. Many thanks for the guidance and support of these professors, colleagues, and friends.

I owe thanks to people from the second time period as well. My initial editor at the Johns Hopkins University Press, Claire McCabe Tamberino, supported my early work and pushed it forward. I appreciate her willingness to take a chance on a new author. My second editor, Henry Tom, led me through the publication process and stood by my work. Meg Wilkes Karaker reviewed several drafts of my manuscript. I appreciate her constructive and encouraging comments, which greatly strengthened the book.

Thank you to LuAnn Albanese, who offered me confidence that the manuscript would be accessible to a varied audience. Thanks to Katie Parkin for commenting on chapter 2 and helping a sociologist write like a historian. My writing was also facilitated by a course release in fall 2006. Thank you to the Department of Political Science, the

Dean's Office, and the Provost's Office at Monmouth University for making that happen. This work was supported in part by a Grant-in-Aid for Creativity Award from Monmouth University.

I owe gratitude beyond words to Johanna Foster, who made the time to read, help reorganize, and edit numerous drafts of this book. I could not have asked for a better colleague or friend to help me through the process.

Many people have bridged both time periods, including numerous family members and friends. My father-in-law offered unwavering interest and confidence in my work. My sisters never asked too many questions but were always there for support. My parents served as a sounding board throughout the entire research and writing process. My father asked questions that pushed my work forward. My mother provided invaluable advice and encouragement. I am fortunate to have easy access to such an established writer and academic. I thank her for helping me navigate the research and publication process.

Maxine Baca Zinn has served as my mentor and advisor throughout my graduate and academic career. She has pushed me to intellectual levels that were sometimes painful to reach but always worthwhile. She has put endless hours into commenting on the drafts of what ultimately became this book. I cannot thank her enough for her confidence in my work and for her encouragement and support over the past fifteen years.

Finally, I thank my immediate family. My children, Jack and Sophie, kept me grounded in reality and reminded me of the important things in life. I could not have completed this work without the help, love, and support of my partner, Karen Diehl. She was a driving force in my decision to become a mother and has always been willing to pick up the slack at home when my professional life consumes my time. She patiently and graciously holds our family together, creates time and space for me to do my work, and provides emotional support to keep me sane.

New Choices, New Families

At the Crossroads

When I came out to my parents in the early 1990s, I remember telling my mother that I still wanted to have children. At the time, I hadn't really considered how I might achieve this goal without the help of a male partner. But I had always wanted children and did not consider my sexual identity a barrier to becoming a mother.

In hindsight, I see that my confidence that as a lesbian I would still be able to parent most likely lay in my class and race privilege. As a White woman coming from an upper-middle-class family, I had never faced any serious obstacles in achieving my goals. My parents, having a progressive mindset, had equipped my three sisters and me with the material means and self-confidence we needed to succeed.

My parents provided good role models for their children. They immigrated to the United States as part of the Jewish Diaspora of World War II, overcoming many economic and social hurdles. They both worked hard. My father became a physician, and my mother became a top professor in the field of nursing. So it is not surprising that, at the time of my coming out, my sisters and I were well on the way to becoming professionals ourselves in assorted fields. And it is also not surprising that even though I came out during a time when options were only recently becoming available to lesbians who wanted to become mothers, my sexual identity did not prevent me from fulfilling my desire to become a parent.

My race and class privilege, however, did not outweigh my sociological training, which made obvious to me the many forms of discrimination and oppression, as well as privilege, that structures of race, class, gender, and sexuality create. As a graduate student I became increasingly interested in studying structural inequalities, particularly from a multiracial feminist perspective. Multiracial feminism is a social structural and social constructionist approach that "challenge[s] the hegemony of feminisms constructed primarily around the lives of white middle-class women" (Baca Zinn and Dill, 1996, p. 323). Rather than thinking about women as a cohesive group, multiracial feminism places difference at the center of its analysis to examine how women are dissimilar from one another based on race and class. Just as feminism critiques mainstream sociology for marginalizing women, multiracial feminism critiques earlier feminisms for making invisible and distorting the lives of women of color (Baca Zinn and Dill, 1996).

When I approached the chair of my dissertation committee with my proposed doctoral study, she suggested I talk with Marilyn Frye, a professor of philosophy whose work focuses on the oppression of women in general and lesbians more specifically. I had never studied under Frye, but I had read her work extensively and had had several informal conversations with her. As I sat in her office discussing possible dissertation topics, Frye asked me why I was interested in studying lesbian motherhood. Why, she asked, are so many researchers assuming that all lesbians want to become mothers? What about the lesbians who do not want to become mothers? Why as feminist researchers do we continue to conflate womanhood (even lesbian womanhood) with motherhood?

Frye's questions, along with my commitment to multiracial feminism and my own experiences, led me to ask three questions about lesbians and motherhood. First, I asked the very basic question of why so many lesbians were choosing motherhood in the mid- to late 1990s. What made this historical moment the "right" time for the emergence of the lesbian baby boom (Lewin, 1993; O'Sullivan, 1995;

Weston, 1991)? Second, I wanted to know how lesbians' mothering decisions (i.e., their decisions to become mothers or remain childfree) are rooted in social and personal processes and not simply based on a "biological clock." Third, I wanted to know what role race, class, gender, and sexuality play in shaping those processes.

As I asked these questions, my research landed in a wonderful place at the crossroads of several key sociological phenomena: the crossroads of motherhood, identity, and the creation of new American families; the crossroads of social and cultural conditions and how they interact with human behavior and choices; the crossroads of race, class, gender, and sexuality; the crossroads of assumed biological mandates and socially constructed processes; and the crossroads of the lesbian community, in which lesbians are at times divided as they debate among themselves the politics and consequences of lesbian motherhood.

By examining lesbians' mothering decisions, this book takes a fresh look at motherhood, personal identity, and the question of choice and free will. It does so by questioning assumptions about motherhood and providing an in-depth look at how lesbians negotiate and participate in the material and ideological systems that both support and hinder their decision-making processes. This book not only examines the contested terrain in which contemporary families are changing; it also informs us of how the very substance of contemporary life—with all its complexities and controversies—is continuously constructed and reconstructed through the interplay between social and personal conditions. And it does so by moving away from White middle-class models as well as from the assumption that all lesbians, as women, want to become mothers.

THE NEW SUBTLE REVOLUTION

American families have been changing dramatically over the past thirty to forty years. As we have moved from an industrial to a postindustrial, global economy, we have seen an increased service sector, decreased manufacturing sector, and the movement of factories and jobs to overseas sites (Eitzen and Baca Zinn, 2006). The changing economy, coupled with several major social movements such as the Civil Rights, Women's, and Gay Liberation movements, has created significant change in the structure of American families. Dual-income-earning families, single-parent families, divorced and blended families, as well as lesbian and gay families are much more prevalent than the idealized father-breadwinner, mother-homemaker, economically independent family—the so-called traditional nuclear family—that many Americans believe is the only proper and productive type of family to have. In fact, according to data collected from the U.S. Census Bureau, in 2002 only 7 percent of U.S. households actually followed the idealized family model, and only 13 percent of married-couple households followed this model (Ameristat, 2003).

Many of the concerns about the changing "American family" revolve around the role of women as mothers: working mothers, single mothers, teen mothers, lesbian mothers. In her 1985 book *Hard Choices: How Women Decide about Work, Career, and Motherhood,* Kathleen Gerson wrote that she was studying a "subtle revolution" concerning the "far reaching changes taking place in the work and family patterns of American women" (p. 1). Shortly after Gerson wrote those words, the United States began facing a second subtle revolution that also concerns far reaching changes taking place in family patterns of American women. This new subtle revolution, known as the "lesbian baby boom" or "gayby boom" (Lewin, 1993; O'Sullivan, 1995; Weston, 1991), has been forming over the past twenty to thirty years. It started with women who became mothers within heterosexual identities and then later identified as lesbians. More recently, women within their identities as lesbians have been choosing motherhood by adopting and birthing children and becoming foster parents (Lewin, 1993; Silber, 1991). At the turn of the millennium, an estimated 22 percent of partnered lesbians had children in their homes, with several million children living in lesbian and gay families (Black et al., 2000; Stacey and Biblarz, 2001).

What is so revolutionary about the emergence of lesbian motherhood, and what distinguishes it from other forms of motherhood, is the speed at which it has developed and the effect it has had on society's understanding of lesbians, motherhood, and family. Until about twenty to thirty years ago, the idea of "lesbian mothers" was an oxymoron (Lewin, 1993; Stacey, 1996; J. M. Thompson, 2002). Women were either mothers or they were lesbians—but they were rarely, if ever, both. Today, as more and more lesbians are provided with new choices, created in part by increased access to reproductive technologies and laws protecting same-sex parents, lesbians are becoming mothers and forming new families in astonishing numbers. In doing so, they are changing the definition of "family," a change that is fueling heated debates about motherhood and families in the United States.

DECISION MAKING WITHIN A CONTEXT OF MIXED MESSAGES

Sociologists have long noted the distinction between beliefs and reality. Oftentimes what we believe is or should be true does not exist in any real way. The ways in which we think about womanhood, motherhood, and family are no exceptions. Beliefs about what makes a "real" woman often lead us toward popular assumptions that all women are "naturally" nurturing, loving, and caring—and that all women, therefore, want to be and will become mothers. The conflation of woman with mother, or the "mandate for motherhood," has long been analyzed and critiqued by feminist researchers (Rich, 1976). The "mandate for motherhood" is the cultural conditioning and encouraging of women to become mothers based on the belief that women do not fulfill their proper and natural roles as women unless they become mothers. We see this mandate exercised in most arenas of women's lives. Girls are given dolls to nurture early in their childhoods. Teachers and parents encourage women to accept less interesting jobs in the workforce, thus subtly encouraging them to choose children over work. Religious doctrines preach the importance and sacredness of motherhood. Media glorify images of motherhood and show negative images of childfree women as "sad spinsters" or "neurotic" career women. Family members directly pressure their daughters, sisters, and nieces to have children (Bartlett, 1994). And laws offer tax breaks to families with children, thus supporting the mandate for motherhood (Faux, 1984).

Despite its prevalence, the mandate for motherhood is enforced only for *some* women. Historically, many groups of women, particularly poor women, women of color, unmarried women, young women, and lesbians have been excluded from the mandate. Until about twenty years ago no one expected lesbians to become mothers. Because lesbians are usually not involved in intimate heterosexual relationships, people never considered them to be mothers. The fact that lesbians did not become mothers was one of the sources of their exclusion from the very category of "woman" (Lewin, 1995a). This separate categorization allowed physicians, mental health professionals, and the courts to pathologize lesbians. So when lesbians did start to become parents in the 1970s and 1980s, many people saw them as "unfit" mothers (DiLapi, 1989; Thompson, 2002). The only true "fit" mothers, according to our popular beliefs and the ensuing public policy, are heterosexual women in married, nuclear families. To complicate matters, popular wisdom has it that if we move away from the married, heterosexual, nuclear family, then the very fabric of society is compromised and there will be a proliferation of social problems among our youth such as increased drug abuse, high school dropouts, violence, and mental health problems (Popenoe, 1993; Whitehead, 1993). The current political efforts to create laws that encourage women to marry, to discourage girls and women from engaging in premarital sex, and to secure marriage as a heterosexual institution are evidence of the strength of this popular "wisdom."

When lesbians start entering into the institution of motherhood, when they actually become mothers without legally marrying and without any sexual contact with men, when lesbians, as women, choose not to become mothers at all, they shake up the very understanding of what it means to be a woman, what it means to be a lesbian, what it means to be a mother, and what it means to have a family (Sullivan, 2004; J. M. Thompson, 2002; Weston, 1991). Lesbians with and without children are creating families that deny every aspect of what our major social institutions such as family, education, religion, law, medicine, politics, and media have taught us to believe to be the only legitimate family form. Therefore, while lesbians have been forming families both with and without children over the past twenty to thirty years, they have been doing so within an often contradictory social and cultural climate. On the one hand, certain social and cultural factors such as the advancement of women's and lesbian, gay, bisexual, and transgender (LGBT) rights, and the widespread use of reproductive technologies have created a climate that facilitates and supports the creation of lesbian families. On the other hand, lesbians are creating families within a heterosexist and homophobic climate fueled by conservative political and religious leaders, as well as by a handful of social scientists. Although lesbians have created their own cultural norms and institutions, like other minority groups they also exist within the dominant heterosexual society that has its own set of norms, values, and institutions. And like other minorities, lesbians must develop a "double consciousness" (DuBois, 1903/1989), a way of understanding and negotiating the contradictory cultures in which they exist.

Even as the effects of the lesbian baby boom sweep across the cultural landscape, lesbians themselves are divided as to their acceptance of the changes that motherhood brings to their own communities and society at large. Some believe that lesbians are transforming the institution of motherhood in wonderful ways; others believe that lesbian mothers are assimilating into a heterosexual and patriarchal institution in an effort to gain heterosexual privilege (Hequembourg, 2007; Lewin, 1993, 1994, 1995a). Those who see lesbian mothers as transforming motherhood look at how lesbians develop more effective parenting skills and create a more egalitarian division of labor than their heterosexual counterparts (Flaks et al., 1995; Sullivan, 1996). They also argue that because lesbians do not need to engage in physical, emotional, or sexual relations with men to have a family, lesbians bypass the traditional patriarchal family (Hequembourg, 2007; Lewin, 1995a).

Lesbians who view lesbian motherhood as a form of assimilation, on the other hand, argue that lesbian mothers perpetuate the belief that all women want to have children. They also gain heterosexual privilege, allowing them to hide their sexual identity behind their status as mothers. Supporters of the assimilationist view argue that many lesbian mothers are playing into traditional definitions of family, particularly if they enter a legal battle after a lesbian couple separates. In such cases, biological and/or legal mothers are winning many custody cases by arguing that they are the only "real" parents of the children (Hequembourg, 2007; Lewin, 1994, 1995). Thus, lesbian mothers are not only gaining privilege, but they are using legal systems to uphold traditional definitions of the family.

Immersed in this cultural landscape, both within lesbian communities and larger American society, lesbians who are thinking about becoming mothers must consider what it means to be a lesbian, to be a woman, to be a mother, and the consequences of their decisions. All these considerations vary significantly among different groups of lesbians because lesbians are a diverse group of people. Lesbians' experiences and identities are shaped by many factors, including race and class (Greene, 1998; Kennedy and Davis, 1993). Even the sexual behavior of lesbians can vary greatly, sometimes being asexual (Rothblum and Brehony, 1993) or including relationships with men (Rust, 1992). Given all these complexities, lesbians make mothering decisions on rocky and often contradictory terrain. Beliefs about motherhood, the promise of reproductive technologies, and progressive laws that allow lesbians to develop and support their families intersect with the simultaneous heterosexist and homophobic backlash against same-sex families, sending a constant flow of mixed messages to lesbians. Understanding the complexities of the changing American family, as well as the mixed messages and ensuing debates and policies affecting family change, allows us to understand the social and cultural turmoil in which lesbians are making mothering decisions.

BETWEEN FREE WILL AND INEVITABILITY

What I have found particularly interesting is that the literature on lesbian motherhood has in many ways overlooked the social and cultural turmoil in which lesbians are making mothering decisions by ignoring the very basic question of *why* lesbians are choosing motherhood. By not asking this question, scholars are implicitly assuming that lesbians, by virtue of being women, "naturally" want to become mothers if given the opportunity. At the same time, they are focusing on how lesbians make intentional decisions, a focus that rests on the assumption that lesbians' decisions to become mothers are fully within their control or based on their free will.

When Marilyn Frye asked me why I was interested in studying lesbian motherhood, what she was really asking was why scholars assume that once lesbians have options to become mothers, they will automatically want to become mothers just because they are women. Just as we assume that all heterosexual women "naturally" want to have children—and that heterosexual women who do not want children are "unnatural" or "unwomanly"—scholars are now eager to assume that because lesbians are women who have access to donor insemination and adoption, then they too must "naturally" want to become mothers. We see this assumption in the recent scholarly and popular literature on lesbian mothers, which rarely questions why lesbians are becoming mothers or why some lesbians are not becoming mothers. Without placing lesbian motherhood within a social, cultural, and personal context, and perhaps in an eager move away from the assumption that "lesbian mother" is an oxymoron, scholars have ignored how lesbians' decisions are socially constructed.

One reason scholars have not thoroughly and critically examined the basic, and yet complex, question as to why lesbians are choosing motherhood is that they are focusing on the *intentional* nature of lesbians' decisions to mother. For lesbians who within their identities as lesbians decide to mother, there are few unwanted or accidental pregnancies or adoptions (Chabot, 1998; Stacey, 1996). By the very nature of lesbian relationships, the desire to have children and the process of becoming a mother requires that lesbians "construct their chosen family forms with an exceptional degree of reflection and intentionality" (Stacey, 1996, p. 111). Lesbians are forced to consider and negotiate every step of the process to becoming mothers, from finding a willing partner or deciding to be a single mother, to coming out to family members and friends, to choosing a method of becoming a mother, to actually obtaining a child. Within the negotiation of numerous social and personal factors, children are intentionally born or adopted into lesbian families.

The creation of intentional families is not unique to lesbian mothers. Childfree lesbians, gay men, and infertile heterosexual women and men also intentionally create families out of friends, "fictive kin", family of origin, and through adoption and the use of reproductive technologies (Weston, 1991). But the unique aspect of creating families through motherhood is that lesbians who intentionally choose to mother must negotiate great political, legal, financial, medical, ideo-logical, and personal challenges to fulfill their mothering desires. As Judith Stacey notes, "Fully intentional childbearing outside of hetero-sexual unions represents one of the only new, truly original, and de-cidedly controversial genres of family formation" (1996, p. 110).

Although I do not question the importance that intentionality plays in lesbians' decisions to become mothers, by focusing on intentional-ity we have forgotten that even though lesbians do not become moth-ers by accident, they do not make mothering decisions within a social and cultural vacuum. Just as heterosexual women make mothering decisions within larger social processes (Gerson, 1985), so do lesbians. These processes have perhaps been hidden because the research to date has focused primarily on White, middle-class lesbians who face fewer social barriers than less privileged working-class lesbians and lesbians of color.

By juxtaposing the placid acceptance that lesbians as women must want to become mothers next to the issue of intentionality, the litera-ture presents an interesting paradox of natural paths versus intentional decision making based on free will. This paradox raises the question of how intentional is lesbians' decision making. One way to answer this question is to look at lesbians' mothering decisions in a com-prehensive, complex, and critical way, and to compare the decision-making processes of childfree lesbians with those of lesbian mothers. In doing so, we can ask a variety of questions. How free from outside social and cultural forces are lesbians when they decide to mother or not to mother? Do lesbians remain childfree because of the historical separation of lesbian and mother? Do they remain childfree because they cannot afford reproductive technologies or adoption costs? Do they remain childfree because of heterosexist ideology that is difficult to counter? Do they remain childfree because of their own ideological or personal desires not to have children? Similarly, do lesbians choose to become mothers so they can hide their sexual identities behind their identities as mothers, moving them from "unnatural lesbian" to "natural, adult, woman-mother" (Lewin, 1995a; Weston, 1991)? Do they become mothers because they are beginning to the feel the same pressure from their families as other (heterosexual) women feel? Do they become mothers in order for their relationship to work or because of their partners' desires (Gerson, 1985)? How much of anyone's mothering decision is really a question of biology, intentional choice or free will, or outside social and personal conditions?

By not asking these questions, the literature to date—as rich and informative as it is—has been limited in its examination of decision-making processes among all women, regardless of sexual identity. The literature has thus implicitly reinforced the belief that becoming a mother is a "natural" choice, while simultaneously assuming that all women, including lesbians, have free will outside of social processes to decide to become mothers or remain childfree. In trying to answer some of these questions, this book begins to fill the gap in the literature by looking at lesbians' decision-making processes, thereby making a significant contribution to the small body of research focusing on the social processes of mothering decisions in general.

PLAN OF THE BOOK

I have grounded this book in multiracial feminism, a perspective that I weave throughout the chapters to explain the social processes lesbians go through to become mothers or remain childfree. In chapter 2 I provide a historical overview of the social conditions and movements that have allowed lesbian families to develop at this historical moment. I do so to help the reader understand why lesbians are presently able to make mothering decisions at all, decisions that were virtually unheard of only twenty or thirty years ago. In this chapter I discuss the ways in which the Gay Liberation Movement, second-wave feminism and the Women's Liberation Movement, the HIV/AIDS epidemic, and the increased use of reproductive and conceptive technologies such as donor insemination and in vitro fertilization (IVF) have created fertile ground in which lesbians can make mothering decisions.

Chapter 3 tells the story of how I recruited a diverse sample of lesbians and collected the ethnographic data that provide the foundation for most of this book. This chapter also allows me to explain how I defined my terms and categories of women. Equally important, in this chapter I introduce the women whose voices we hear throughout the following chapters.

Drawing on these voices, Chapter 4 looks at the first phase of the decision-making process by examining how lesbians' childhood experiences, primarily within their families of origin, shape their early desires to become mothers or remain childfree. This chapter looks at key social and cultural conditions that shape lesbians' desires including childhood experiences, lesbians' interpretations of their own mothers' relationships to their families and the paid labor force, and gender and racial discrimination.

Chapters 5 through 8 discuss the second, and larger, phase of the decision-making process by focusing on four key factors that lesbians must consider in their decisions to become mothers or remain childfree. These factors both support and constrain the transformation of lesbians' mothering *desires* (i.e., whether they *want* to become mothers or remain childfree) into mothering *decisions* (i.e., whether they actually become mothers or remain childfree). Chapters 5 though 8 place the voices and experiences of the women I interviewed within a multiracial feminist framework to explain of how race, class, gender, and sexuality shape lesbians' mothering decisions. In these chapters I also draw on previous research to provide an understanding of a broader spectrum of lesbians' experiences and to explain my findings.

Chapter 5, in particular, discusses the first key factor that lesbians must weigh in making mothering decisions. This chapter explains how lesbians sift through their own beliefs about motherhood to figure out whether they will become mothers or remain childfree. This chapter looks at how some lesbians reject pregnancy and adoption, thus greatly restricting their options for becoming mothers. It also looks at how lesbians with negative views of lesbian motherhood are most likely to remain childfree. Similarly, having a positive view of lesbian motherhood allows lesbians to consider motherhood in ways that they may not have within heterosexual relationships. I discuss how some lesbians in the study "swore up and down" that they would not become mothers because to them motherhood meant women's oppression and the thwarting of educational and career goals. However, as they entered into lesbian relationships, they realized they could create egalitarian and flexible families, characteristics that encouraged some lesbians to become mothers.

Chapter 6 looks at the importance of lesbian support networks and communities and how they shape lesbians' decision-making processes. Because lesbian communities are divided not only by mothering decision but also by race and class, lesbians must negotiate their place in lesbian communities. Their negotiation helps them determine what part of the community they can and want to fit into and how much support they will receive in their mothering decisions. Furthermore, for lesbians who want to become mothers, being connected to lesbian mother networks is critical in accessing physicians and sperm banks that are willing to work with lesbians.

Chapter 7 discusses how, in making their mothering decisions, lesbians weigh the support and constraints that intimate partners provide. Intimate partners play an important role in encouraging lesbians to choose motherhood or remain childfree. For some lesbians, a partner wanting children is often enough to turn a childfree desire into a decision to mother. Similarly, finding a partner who already has children or who does not want children is, at times, enough to keep an ambivalent lesbian, or even a lesbian who wants to mother, childfree. This chapter also discusses how some lesbians make mothering decisions outside of any partner considerations.

Chapter 8 examines the fourth factor that affects lesbians' decision-making processes, specifically, how lesbians consider the benefits and barriers presented by work that support or constrain their personal goals, including their desires to become mothers or remain childfree. Although literature on women's employment often focuses on how the linkage between work and family is one the greatest challenges women face *after* a child arrives, as in research conducted on heterosexual women, the lesbians I interviewed discussed how work is one of the most important factors influencing their decisions as to whether or not a child *will* arrive. Work is an important factor because it presents lesbians with a variety of conditions that at times directly supports lesbians' mothering desires but at other times constrains those desires, thus causing women to shift their mothering decisions. Two types of support and constraints—the chance to be upwardly mobile and the lack of health insurance and domestic partner benefits—encourage lesbians to remain childfree. Two other types—having flexible and established careers and having unfulfilling jobs—encourage lesbians to become mothers. This chapter looks specifically at how class and race shape the different types of support and constraints that work creates, and how lesbians consider the benefits and barriers of work so that they can achieve existing personal goals, or create new personal goals, including becoming mothers or remaining childfree.

The concluding chapter, chapter 9, revisits the question of intentionality to look at how lesbians wade through social and cultural conditions to make their mothering decisions. It also revisits the major themes—making decisions within the context of mixed messages, the socially constructed nature of mothering decisions, and the importance of using a multiracial feminist perspective—to look at what we can learn from lesbians' decision-making processes. The chapter concludes by looking at how lesbians' mothering decisions fit squarely within a broader context of the changing nature of American families and how studying lesbian decision-making processes and lesbian families in general informs the larger study of all American families.

CHAPTER TWO

The Historical Rise of Lesbian Families

Although I am not a historian, I am mindful that every social phenomenon builds upon events, conditions, and beliefs that continuously develop out of our past. In reading the literature on lesbian motherhood and in speaking with lesbians themselves, I began to see that many of the issues lesbians discuss come out of a recent, rich, and critical history that has allowed them to make mothering decisions and form families in a particular way at this historical moment. In conducting my research, I became interested in the question of why lesbian families developed at this specific moment in time. What factors have come together to enable the development of lesbian families and lesbians' options to become mothers? The rise of lesbian families is a historically recent phenomenon. Although women have lived and participated in same-sex relationships for hundreds of years, lesbian families as a distinct social category have developed only during the past three decades. Because the history is so recent, answering questions about the rise of lesbian families and lesbian motherhood is critical to understanding the current processes lesbians go through in making their mothering decisions.

Historically speaking, it is difficult to separate the growth of lesbian families from that of gay male families. However, because I specifically address lesbian decision-making and the formation of lesbian families in this book, this chapter speaks largely to the history of lesbian families, and not gay male families. Lesbian families emerged at the end of the twentieth century out of four key factors: (1) the development of an organized Gay Liberation Movement, (2) second-wave feminism and the Women's Rights Movement, (3) the HIV/AIDS epidemic, and (4) the development of reproductive and conceptive technologies. Although these are not the only factors, they were central to bringing lesbian families to the fore of public attention and have greatly influenced the new visibility and cultural understanding of lesbians, gays, and their families (D'Emilio, 1983, 1993; Morningstar, 1999; Pollack, 1995; Purcell, 1998; Stacey, 1998). Focusing on the historical rise of lesbian families allows us to understand how lesbians can currently decide if they want to become mothers or remain childfree.

THE DEVELOPMENT OF THE GAY LIBERATION MOVEMENT

Today, terms such as *same-sex marriage, civil unions, lesbian families,* and *lesbian mothers* are fairly common in American vocabulary. None of these terms would have existed without the efforts of lesbians and gay men who fought for recognition and personal rights throughout the twentieth century. Prior to the twentieth century, same-sex behavior existed, but the current identities (i.e., lesbian, gay) associated with those behaviors did not. In fact, *heterosexual* and *homosexual* are terms that come out of the distinction between same-sex and opposite-sex attractions and behaviors that people began to make only within the past 100 to 150 years (Katz, 1996; Weeks, 2003). The formation of sexual identities is closely tied to the Homophile Movement of the first half of the twentieth century and the Gay Liberation Movement of the latter half of the century. And the formation of the Gay Liberation Movement was a key factor in the formation of lesbian families and the lesbian baby boom.

In the first half of the twentieth century, when industrialization, urbanization, and World War II created opportunities for sex-segregated organizations, women and men began forming homosexual identities (D'Emilio, 1983, 1993). During the 1950s, mostly middle-class White homosexuals began to organize what historians call the Homophile

Movement, forming groups such as the Mattachine Society and the Daughters of Bilitis. The purpose of such groups was to help homosexuals connect with other homosexuals and to fight against sexual discrimination (D'Emilio, 1983). Homosexuals also began to enjoy a social life, particularly in bars and at private parties, although they segregated themselves by race and class (Kennedy and Davis, 1993). Despite the formation of early political groups and social activities, "the prevailing view of homosexuals and lesbians as essentially flawed individuals, responsible for their predicament, inhibited the development of a group consciousness" and a mass movement (D'Emilio, 1983, p. 129).

It was not until the early 1960s that gays developed such a mass movement. One critical spark was a court case that banned censorship of pornographic and homosexual materials. From the 1930s to the 1950s, government agencies, including the courts and the police, actively censored written materials and films containing "obscenities." Homosexual materials were specific targets in the censorship campaign. The 1957 *Roth v. United States* decision of the U.S. Supreme Court changed the definition of what materials could be censored (D'Emilio, 1983). Looser guidelines on censorship in the 1960s facilitated a growth of lesbian and male homosexual literature and films that placed homosexuals in a more positive light, rather than following the medical model of homosexuality as a sickness. Not only did the literature and films offer positive role models, but they also helped homosexuals recognize that there were many people like them throughout the United States. The growth of mass media focusing on homosexuality fueled the movement, providing the resources lesbians and gays needed to form and find their own subculture (D'Emilio, 1983).

Another factor that fueled the Gay Liberation Movement was a change in social science thinking about homosexuals. Whereas previous work by sexologists and other social scientists saw homosexuality as a psychological illness, a new group of scholars—including some social scientists, gay and lesbian scholars primarily from the humanities, and radical feminists—began to understand homosexuality within a socially constructed framework (D'Emilio, 1983; Stein and Plummer, 1994). Alfred Kinsey and his colleagues' 1948 and 1954 publications were among the first studies to challenge previous ideas about homosexuality. Kinsey's studies showed that men and women engaged in a wider range of homosexual behaviors than previously thought. Also in the 1950s, psychologist Evelyn Hooker, who worked in the field of mental health, showed "that there were no discernable differences between the psychological testing profiles of gay men and heterosexual men" (Cabaj, 1998, pp. 12–13).

During the 1960s, new ways of thinking about homosexuality continued to arise. Rising out of the emerging Women's Rights Movement, lesbian feminists began making connections between sexuality and power. They argued that society is based on a system of "compulsory heterosexuality" policed by social institutions that force people to be heterosexual (Rich, 1993). Starting in the late 1970s and continuing throughout the 1980s, lesbian feminists continued to push the study of lesbians to a new level (Escoffier, 1992). However, because feminists tended to see sexuality as part of gender, they generally did not try to understand how sexuality might also be separate from gender. In contrast, gay and lesbian studies scholars began thinking about sexuality outside of a gender framework. Many of these scholars came out of the "the Stonewall generation" of the late 1960s, when gay liberationists and feminist activists brought their perspectives into an academic setting (Escoffier, 1992). Gay and lesbian studies evolved into "queer studies" during the late 1980s (Epstein, 1994; Stein and Plummer, 1994) and was associated with grassroots activist groups such as Queer Nation and ACT UP.

From the late 1970s throughout the 1980s, queer studies scholars began questioning a variety of sexual categories, such as heterosexual, homosexual, gay, lesbian, and bisexual (Butler, 1993; Sedgwick, 1993). They argued that because we tend to see categories as opposites (e.g., heterosexual and homosexual), we lose sight of how fluid, changeable, and socially constructed these categories really are. Queer theorists also looked at how issues of sexuality and power exist even in places where most people think they are absent. They questioned heterosexual power relations that define homosexuality. In fact, queer theory has become a popular academic field today precisely because it places diverse sexualities at the center of its analysis and legitimizes the lives of lesbians and gays.

Along with queer theory, the sociological study of sexualities, and particularly of homosexuality as a social construct, began to gain ground in the early 1970s, when sociologists began to think about homosexuality within a "deviance" framework (Stein and Plummer, 1994). Sociologists defined deviance not as "a quality of the act the person commits, but rather [as] a consequence of the application by other of rules and sanctions to an 'offender'" (Howard Becker, 1963, as cited in D'Emilio, 1983, p. 142). In this way, sociologists began to see homosexuals as regular people who were treated differently because they deviated from the dominant sexual norm. By placing homosexuality within a deviance framework, sociologists offered a positive way of looking at homosexuality that focused on group social life and "identified the 'problem' as one caused by society, not by the homosexual or lesbian" (D'Emilio, 1983, p. 144). Academics contributed, therefore, to changing cultural ideas of what it means to be homosexual. Perhaps not so coincidently, given social science rethinking and the ongoing Gay Liberation Movement, in 1973 the American Psychiatric Association removed homosexuality from the *Diagnostic and Statistical Manual of Mental Disorders (DSM) III*.

A third factor that sparked an organized Gay Liberation Movement was the Black Civil Rights Movement. The Civil Rights Movement showed homosexuals of diverse racial-ethnic backgrounds how ordinary men and women could organize a mass movement to fight against oppression (D'Emilio, 1983). Around the country, White homosexual organizations began modeling their actions after the actions of Black organizations to create a more radical homophile movement. Drawing on the example of confrontational groups such as the Black Panthers, the Nation of Islam, and the Congress of Racial Equality, homosexuals developed a new culture of protest, one that moved away from a strategy of equality through the courts to one of community organizing (D'Emilio, 1983). The Civil Rights Movement, in conjunction with the 1970s Women's Rights Movement, gave lesbians of color in particular a new understanding about the intersections of different oppressions, thus broadening the various social movements of the time to include multiple types of oppression, such as race, class, gender, and sexuality (Lorde, 1984; Smith, 1998).

In addition to influencing the organizations and strategies of homophile groups, the Civil Rights Movement helped people form strong homosexual identities. As with Black heterosexuals, the Civil Rights Movement gave Black homosexuals a Black identity. Developing an identity is something that Black gays and lesbians had continuously fought to incorporate into the largely White Homophile Movement. Furthermore, just as their Black counterparts began to use skin color as a source of pride, homosexuals of diverse racial backgrounds began to think of their sexuality as a source of pride. Perhaps it was this new sense of pride that spurred homosexuals to revolt against police riots at the Stonewall Bar in New York City in 1969, which marked the end of the Homophile Movement and the beginning of the modern Gay Liberation Movement (D'Emilio, 1983; Faderman, 1991).

As the Gay Liberation Movement provided a new sense of pride, lesbians and gay men no longer felt the need to so carefully hide their sexual identities and therefore began to "come out" or reveal their sexual identities to those around them. In fact, coming out became a political strategy of the movement. By coming out to family and friends, lesbians and gays became more visible, more vulnerable to attack, and therefore more invested in the fight for equality and legal recognition (D'Emilio, 1983). As a political strategy, however, coming out has experienced limited success because the process has been, and remains, a difficult one. Coming out requires that people go against dominant beliefs and the policies that enforce those beliefs, that heterosexuality is the only good, healthy, and natural way to be (G. Rubin, 1993).

Coming out has been particularly difficult for people in subordinate race and class positions because of historical race and class relations in the United States. For example, because the sexuality of Blacks has been racially stigmatized and abused by Whites, Blacks have overcompensated by following more puritan beliefs that encourage homophobia (Clarke, 1983; Greene, 1998). This has been particularly true for middle-class Blacks who have felt "the need to prove that they are 'just as nice as those white folks'" (Cathy J. Cohen, 1996, p. 376, as cited in Kennamer et al., 2000). Homophobia in Black communities and families has been, therefore, partially a product of racism. To deflect some of the racialized sexuality back onto White culture, communi-

ties of color have invoked racial images of their own by saying that
"lesbianism" is a "White disease," not a problem indigenous to their
own cultures (Clarke, 1983; Espín, 1997; Loiacano, 1989; Morales,
1990; Silvera, 1995; Smith, 1998). Such views continue to make it very
difficult for lesbians of color to come out.

Coming out has also been historically complicated because families of color are tightly interconnected with larger communities of
color. For many people of color, regardless of sexual identity, the racial-
ethnic community in which they grew up is a primary reference point,
a haven against a racist world, and a source of economic and emotional support (Anzaldúa, 1987; Espín, 1997; hooks, 1989; Loiacano,
1989; Moraga, 1997; Morales, 1990; Silvera, 1995; B. Smith, 1983). For
lesbians of color, coming out to the family has not only jeopardized
intrafamily relationships but has also threatened their strong association with their ethnic community. As a result, minority gays and
lesbians have "run the risk of feeling uprooted as an ethnic person"
(Morales, 1990, p. 233).

Homophobia within communities of color has historically been
tied not only to racism but also to sexism. In Latino communities,
particularly among upper-class Latinos, the honor of the family has
been "strongly tied to the sexual purity of women. And the concept of
honor and dignity is one of the essential distinctive marks of Hispanic
culture" (Espín, 1997, pp. 87–88). Although women have been encouraged to build emotionally close relationships with other women,
Latinos to this day do not consider lesbian relationships to be "sexually
pure" (Espín, 1997). Furthermore, because Latinas are traditionally
not expected to discuss or overtly show or acknowledge their sexual
desires, coming out to family and friends has meant going against
both sexual and gender norms. However, within Latino, as well as
Black, families and communities, there has been, and continues to exist, a "don't ask, don't tell" practice for lesbians who have been willing
to keep their same-sex relationships closeted (Espín, 1997; Greene,
1994; Morales, 1990).

Working-class White lesbians have experienced similar challenges
in coming out. Because working-class White families face greater economic hardship than middle-class families, they have relied heavily

on family relationships for "economic and emotional support against the pressures of labour market and workplace" (Connell et al., 1993, p. 117). The result is that working-class White families have developed a strong ideology based upon traditional notions of family in which there is a clear gender division of labor. As in Latino families, strong gender ideology has translated into strict rules about sexuality for women and men. However, close families have been reluctant to exile their children. So while working-class White families might show displeasure about having a lesbian daughter or gay son, like families of color, they may be flexible enough to adopt a "don't ask, don't tell" practice.

The group for whom coming out has historically and currently been the most successful as a personal and political strategy is middle-class White lesbians. Because middle-class White families have fit into, and in fact have created, most gender and sexual norms, they have not fallen under the same scrutiny as working-class families or families of color. Therefore, race and class privilege have allowed them more flexibility in accepting diverse sexualities than other families. Indeed, even today, Whites are more likely than Latinas to come out to their families, and both groups are more likely to come out than Blacks (Grov et al., 2006; Kennamer et al., 2000). One result of the political strategy of coming out has been an increased visibility of White middle-class lesbians and gays, a visibility that has inadvertently reinforced the idea that homosexuality is a "White disease" not found within communities of color.

A more positive result of the Gay Liberation Movement's strategy of coming out was that those lesbians and gays who did come out continued to develop a sense of pride in their new identities and a sense that they deserved the same rights and level of respect as heterosexuals in the United States. This new sense of self greatly contributed to lesbians, particularly middle-class White lesbians, feeling that they had the right to create families just like their heterosexual counterparts. As they began to feel more comfortable with their newly created families, lesbians and gays began to understand how socially and economically disadvantaged their families were by their not being able to legally marry their partners. The fight for legalized same-sex marriage equality began in the 1970s and has become the Gay Liberation Movement's most important issue in the twenty-first century.

Marriage is an institution with a long history of discrimination that has allowed societies to restrict the rights of women and racial minorities. Currently, political and religious leaders are using marriage to restrict the rights of LGBTs and maintain heterosexuality as the only "normal" and legitimate form of sexuality in the United States. At a time when other industrialized nations—including the Netherlands, Germany, Belgium, Finland, Portugal, France, Hungary, Great Britain, Spain, and Canada (Fish, 2005)—have either legalized same-sex marriage or recognized civil unions, U.S. conservatives are fighting fiercely against any legal national recognition of same-sex couples. Through the rhetoric of the family values debate and the heterosexual marriage movement, conservatives focus on family structure rather than family well-being. They argue that a move away from the "traditional" nuclear family causes a decline in material and economic conditions within U.S. society (Dill, Baca Zinn, and Patton, 1998). Because lesbian families differ from the "traditional" family form, conservatives target lesbian families through policies and rhetoric (Stacey, 1996). Supporters of the heterosexual marriage movement place lesbian and gay families at the heart of their debate and provide policy makers and society in general a platform from which to discriminate against lesbian and gay families.

Exclusion from the legal institution of marriage presents many challenges to lesbian families. Lack of access to child custody for both biological and adoptive parents, lack of medical and financial benefits for partners, and lack of legal recognition of partnerships in hospitals, schools, and financial matters present difficulties for lesbians in maintaining relationships with partners and children. Despite conservative efforts and the force behind the heterosexual marriage movement, the marriage equality movement is equally strong. Although lesbians and gay men began fighting for marital rights in the early 1970s, it was the *Baehr v. Lewin* (and later the *Baehr v. Miike*) case in Hawaii that brought wide political attention and media coverage to the issue of same-sex marriage in the 1990s (Lewin, 1998; Mohr, 1994; Tong, 1998). In the 1970s, gays and lesbians challenged marital laws, "claiming that in accordance with common-law tradition, whatever is not prohibited must be allowed" (Mohr, 1994, p. 35). The courts dismissed this challenge, stating that marriage automatically implies

gender difference. Lesbians and gays also challenged courts by referring to the antimiscegenation laws that were nationally abolished in
1967, arguing that preventing marriage based on sexual orientation
was similar to preventing marriage based on race (Lewin, 1998; Tong,
1998). Courts dismissed this challenge as well, until the 1993 *Baehr
v. Lewin* case in Hawaii, which drew parallels to those same antimiscegenation laws (Tong, 1998). In response to this advancement, in
1996 President Clinton signed into law the Defense of Marriage Act
(DOMA), which for the first time specified that marriage could occur
only between a man and a woman.

Given the lack of marriage equality and in an effort to attract and
keep lesbian and gay employees, many companies and state and local
municipalities have instituted domestic partnership programs giving
unmarried couples access to health and other benefits. However, domestic partner benefits provide only localized rights in companies or
municipalities. Supporters of same-sex marriage see these benefits
as "second-class solutions" because they only offer limited benefits to
those living in specific geographical areas (Kendell, 1998, p. 53).

Lesbian and gay activists won a major victory in the summer of
2000, when Vermont instituted the "Civil Union law" that "permits
eligible couples of the same sex to be joined in civil union" (Markovitz,
2000). The law grants same-sex partners in Vermont "all of the state-
level rights and responsibilities of marriage" (HRC, 2004a). Three
years later, on November 18, 2003, deciding on the *Goodridge et al.
v. Department of Public Health* case and handing down the first-of-its-
kind ruling in the United States, the Massachusetts Supreme Court
stated that under their state constitution, same-sex couples must be
given the same rights as opposite-sex couples (HRC, 2004b).

The Gay Liberation Movement made further strides in 2005 when,
following the Vermont model, Connecticut's legislature passed a civil
union bill conferring "all of the state-level spousal rights and responsibilities on parties to a civil union" (Connecticut Substitute Senate Bill
963, 2005, as cited in HRC, 2004c). Similarly, in response to a lawsuit
filed by seven lesbian and gay couples, the New Jersey Supreme Court
ruled in October 2006 that lesbian and gay couples are entitled to
the same legal rights and financial benefits as heterosexual couples.

After the court left it to the legislature to decide what the LGBT unions should be called, in 2007 New Jersey was the third state to institute statewide civil unions. And most recently, in April 2007, New Hampshire's legislature passed a civil union bill that would "permit same-sex couples to enter spousal unions and have the same rights, responsibilities, and obligations under state law as married couples" (HRC, 2007). As I was finishing this book, the bill was awaiting Governor Lynch's signature. Despite the progress that the Gay Liberation Movement has made in the five states mentioned above, forty "states have laws or state constitutional amendments that purport to ban marriage between same-sex couples" (HRC, 2004a). The importance of the few cases of marriage or civil unions notwithstanding, most state and federal laws prohibit same-sex marriage.

The benefits and protection that marriage offers families in general are some of the main reasons why many lesbians and gays want so desperately to be legally married. Marriage secures hospital visitations of a spouse, Social Security benefits, the right of a same-sex partner to immigrate to the United States, health insurance coverage, retirement savings and pension plans, family leave when a spouse is ill, the right to live together in nursing homes, the right to access infertility treatment, the ability for both parents to adopt a child, the protection of child custody, and over a thousand additional benefits (Bolte, 1998; Gomes, 2003; HRC, 2004d; Lewin, 2004). The entitlements of marriage not only provide economic stability to many families, but they also mark family legitimacy and authenticity (Lewin, 2004).

As marriage equality efforts within the Gay Liberation Movement gain momentum, they add to the historical context within which lesbians are deciding to become mothers or remain childfree. If achieved, marriage equality will undoubtedly open the doors for lesbians to not only form legally sanctioned relationships but also to adopt and conceive legally sanctioned and supported children, perhaps lifting some of the barriers lesbians currently face in making their mothering decisions.

FEMINISM AND THE WOMEN'S RIGHTS MOVEMENT

In addition to the development of the Gay Liberation Movement, second-wave feminism and the Women's Rights Movement also broke ground for the formation of lesbian families. These forces gave women new ways of interacting not only with men but also with other women. A combination of factors—including women being able to come out as lesbians, the strong critique of the nuclear family, and the creation of new *heterosexual* family forms—created a space in which lesbians could form families that were not radically different from some of their heterosexual counterparts, thus allowing lesbians for the first time in history to become part of the American family landscape.

Feminists of the 1960s and 1970s strongly condemned the nuclear family for the oppressive nature of its roles for women, particularly as housewives and mothers (Allen, 1983; Firestone, 1970; Giminez, 1983). Questioning gender roles allowed women to think about and explore alternative roles. With women's new consciousness, divorce rates increased, as did the number of women and men living as cohabitants, not as husband and wife. New nonmarital arrangements not only changed the shape of the family but also challenged the idea that sexual relations were only for producing children. Because of these new relationships, starting in the 1970s, "heterosexuality began to look somewhat like homosexuality, as nonreproductive sex and cohabitation without marriage came to be commonplace" (Faderman, 1991, p. 201). By challenging gender roles and sexual norms within families, "feminism helped to remove gay life and gay politics from the margins of American society" (D'Emilio, 1983, p. 237).

In addition, as radical feminists of color began conceptualizing gender as part of a "matrix of domination," a concept more fully explored during the 1980s (Collins, 1990), feminists began challenging the notion of "the monolithic family," which stresses the nuclear family with the male breadwinner and female housekeeper and mother. They began studying families of color and lower-class families to understand how families develop out of economic, social, and cultural inequalities. Feminists examined how society is organized in unequal ways along lines of race, class, gender, and sexuality, to create different family experiences for different groups of people (Thorne, 1992). Although family scholars have only recently begun studying lesbian families, radical feminists of color helped develop the necessary conceptual tools for understanding and socially accepting a variety of family forms within the larger family landscape.

The final way in which second-wave feminism and the Women's Right's Movement helped develop lesbian families was by helping married women with children come out as lesbians. In the 1970s, feminism was a key factor in helping women understand and honor their attractions to other women (Lewin, 1993). A form of radical feminism called lesbian feminism provided a safe space in which women could explore their sexuality, understand the power inequalities within sexual relationships, and create an avenue for women to come out as lesbians. In addition, in connecting personal issues with political ones, many women joined feminist consciousness-raising groups that "had a direct impact on their paths into lesbianism" (Lewin, 1993, p. 20). Some of the women in these groups were already divorced; others were still married. Through the networks created and politics espoused during the feminist movement, some women came out as lesbians and left their husbands. The end result was the first generation of lesbians with children. This early generation of lesbian mothers paved the way for lesbians today to become mothers. The issues that the first generation of lesbian mothers had to deal with, such as fighting child custody battles and proudly placing "lesbian" and "mother" together, have shaped current lesbian family struggles dealing with rights to adopt and parent children, as well as with rights to form legally recognized families through marriage.

THE HIV/AIDS EPIDEMIC

In addition to the Gay Liberation Movement, second-wave feminism, and the Women's Rights Movement, the HIV/AIDS epidemic also shaped the development of lesbian families. It is no accident that the beginning of the lesbian baby boom coincided with the death of a great number of gay men from AIDS in the 1980s and 1990s. With so many men dying in gay communities, lesbians and gays found that bringing children into those communities was a way to counteract the sense of loss and the fear of disease (Lewin, 1993; Moraga, 1997; Weston, 1991). Bringing children into lesbian and gay communities seemed to be a particularly salient strategy for lesbians and gays of color. During the 1980s, "over 72 percent of AIDS cases occurred in gay/bisexual men and over 41 percent of the total cases [were] ethnic minority group members" (Centers for Disease Control, as cited in Morales, 1990, p. 224). In her memoir of her own "queer" mother-hood, Cherrie Moraga discusses her feelings of devastation and loss as gay Latino men died of AIDS. She asked, "Is there a kind of queer balance to this birthing and dying . . . lesbians giving life to sons, our brothers passing?" (Moraga, 1997, p. 62).

Despite the epidemic's influence on lesbians bringing increas-ing numbers of children into their communities, in the late 1980s through the 1990s lesbians also began distancing themselves from using gay men as sperm donors. Because lesbians feared contracting HIV and passing HIV to a fetus, they became reluctant to ask gay men to donate their sperm. This was an important change to the time prior to the HIV/AIDS epidemic, when lesbians often asked gay men to partner up for procreative purposes. In the 1990s, however, few lesbians were willing to risk exposure to HIV/AIDS. To date, most les-bians find donors through regulated sperm banks that test sperm for an array of diseases (Bernstein and Stephenson, 1995; Stacey, 1996; Sullivan, 2004; Weston, 1991).

The fear and risk of HIV/AIDS not only has reduced gay men's participation in the co-parenting process with lesbians; it also has re-duced the options for lesbians who cannot afford to purchase sperm from sperm banks or pay legal fees for adoption (Weston, 1991). Thus, the HIV/AIDS epidemic has both inspired the lesbian baby boom and limited lesbian (and gay) parenting options.

REPRODUCTIVE AND CONCEPTIVE TECHNOLOGIES

The fourth and final major historical development that helped cre-ate a social space in which lesbian families developed was the increased use of reproductive technologies (Stacey, 1998). The term *reproductive technologies* includes many different techniques of varying degrees of medical intervention, including fertility control technologies, la-bor and childbirth technologies, prenatal and neonatal technologies, and conceptive technologies (Giminez, 1991). The most significant of these for lesbians are conceptive technologies, particularly donor insemination. Conceptive technologies have revolutionized families in general, including lesbian families. Many conceptive technologies, and particularly donor insemination, were originally developed and continue to be used primarily to address male infertility (Lasker, 1998). Because infertile men have long been embarrassed about their infertility, doctors kept donor insemination a medical secret until the 1970s and 1980s, when other reproductive technologies, such as IVF and egg donation, emerged on the public scene.

Although we often think about reproductive technologies as mainly medical techniques, their use rests firmly on labor market trends, pronatalist ideology, and capitalism. The increased use of reproductive technologies occurred in the late twentieth century because women began delaying childbearing in order to get jobs and earn a living in the increasing service economy. As women delayed having children, their fertility levels dropped. At the same time, Americans have held on to the belief that children who are biogenetically connected to their parents are the best kind, and the only "real" kind, of offspring to have (Rothman, 1989; Sullivan, 2004). Lower fertility levels and beliefs about biogenetic connections have translated into the increased use of reproductive technologies to help women get pregnant (Lemonick, 1997; McDaniel, 1996; Rothman, 1989).

Another factor that encouraged the growth of reproductive technologies was capitalism. In the United States, where there is no national health system to regulate such technologies, physicians take advantage of the opportunity to make money by offering reproductive services (Lemonick, 1997; Rothman, 1989). Physicians charge huge fees for conceptive technologies. For example, the average cost for one IVF cycle is approximately $8,000. The cost of more technically complicated procedures is even higher. In addition, the United States is one of the few countries in which people pay for sperm (Blank, 1998). Sperm banks charge over $150 per vial of sperm, plus shipping costs of close to $100 because sperm must be kept frozen during the shipping and storage process. Once lesbians learn of these prices, they often begin to consider other routes to motherhood (Boggis, 2001).

Compounding the issue of cost is the lack of insurance coverage for conceptive technologies. Most insurance companies do not cover the physician fees, the drug treatments associated with the procedures, or the sperm used in conceptive technologies. Companies that do cover such technologies only do so if there is a medical necessity shown through a physician's diagnosis of infertility. However, many lesbians who use conceptive technologies are not infertile but rather do not have access to sperm. Unless physicians are willing to indicate infertility as an official diagnosis, lesbians find it difficult to be reimbursed by their health insurance for infertility treatment (Murphy, 2001).

Despite high costs that discourage less affluent Americans from using conceptive technologies, the combination of American beliefs about biogenetic connections between parent and child and a medical system that allows physicians to offer a variety of services to a wide clientele has led to the creation of over three hundred fertility clinics in the past twenty years. Nearly sixty thousand women a year used conceptive technologies in the late 1990s, resulting in over eleven thousand live births a year (Health Pages, 1996–98).

The increased use of reproductive technologies is fundamentally changing the nature of families and is shaking up the most basic assumptions about families (Eichler, 1996). The use of conceptive technologies that are medically controlled and used primarily in physicians' offices means that women and men are making decisions about bearing children "in a context which dissociates issues relating to fertility and the family from sexual intercourse" (Novaes, 1998, p. 105). Although Americans assume that women conceive children through heterosexual sexual intercourse, many women are conceiving children without sexual intercourse, and in some cases without the presence of a man. Conceptive technologies are also wreaking legal havoc and raising ethical questions about who is the "real" mother (Eichler, 1996; Snowden and Snowden, 1998). Giminez (1991) offers seven different ways that conceptive technologies and surrogacy have shattered the historical unity of being genetically, gestationally, and socially a mother. Because of surrogacy, egg donation, IVF, embryo transfers, and other conceptive technologies, many women can make any combination of genetic, gestational, and social claims to children.

Conceptive technologies have changed the very definitions and understanding of motherhood and of family relationships.

Women's increased use of conceptive technologies has broken ground for the creation of lesbian families. Although married heterosexual couples make up most of the users of such technologies, single heterosexual women and lesbians in the United States are also increasingly using them, particularly donor insemination (Lasker, 1998). Donor insemination is attractive to lesbians because it offers them the chance to have a biogenetically connected child without having sexual relations with a man. As Faderman notes, with "the dual proliferation of the pill and donor insemination . . . [women] no longer [have] to get pregnant as a result of having heterosexual intercourse, and women no longer [have] to have heterosexual intercourse in order to get pregnant" (1997, p. 62). As lesbians increasingly used conceptive technologies, by the late 1990s an estimated ten thousand children were born to lesbians in the United States using donor insemination alone (Lasker, 1998).

The development of the Gay Liberation Movement, second-wave feminism and the Women's Rights Movement, the HIV/AIDS epidemic, and reproductive and conceptive technologies are key historical factors that have led to the rise of lesbian families. If not for these factors, it is unlikely that lesbians would have had any real options for making mothering decisions during the 1990s. Just as these four factors came together at a particular moment in history to create a social space in which a revolutionary family form could develop, they also simultaneously created a social space for the beginning of an emotionally charged discussion about the morality, viability, and long-term consequences of lesbian mothers and their children.

What have been left out of this history, however, are the voices of lesbians themselves discussing how they decide whether they want to become mothers or remain childfree. In the following chapters you will hear their voices and understand how the historical foundation laid down by key factors since at least the mid-1900s have allowed lesbians to make mothering decisions in the late twentieth and early twenty-first centuries.

CHAPTER THREE

Recruiting Lesbian Participants and Collecting Data

When I began my research in 1999, I was both excited and nervous. Excited because I was embarking on an adventure that I hoped would lead to the completion of my doctorate. Nervous because conducting research is hard work that does not always take you where you want to go.

Drawing on the principles of multiracial feminism, I began my research by thinking about how I would collect the data I wanted, how I might go about finding participants who would be willing to share their experiences with me, and what tools I would need to analyze the information they provided. Because my questions involved the nuanced relationships between people and social conditions as shaped by race, class, gender, and sexuality, the research method I chose was necessarily complex. I needed to maximize the information obtained from a small group of participants, to recruit participants from a variety of race and class backgrounds, and to organize the data in a way that reflected the voices and experiences of the women I interviewed. This chapter describes how I set up my research project and how I recruited the women whose voices you will hear throughout the remainder of this book.

DEFINING TERMS AND CATEGORIES

Before beginning my research, I needed to define the categories of women I wanted to include in the study. These categories consisted of lesbians in general, lesbian mothers and childfree lesbians more specifically, and lesbians of diverse racial-ethnic and class backgrounds. It is not easy to define who falls into the category of lesbian. Although the common understanding of lesbians is women who have intimate and sexual relationships exclusively with other women, the sexual experiences of lesbians vary considerably. For example, women who identify as lesbians have many similar sexual experiences as women who identify as bisexual (Rust, 1992). In an attempt to respect the identities of women, and following past research on lesbians, I defined *lesbians* as women who identify themselves as lesbian (Weston, 1991).

I defined *lesbian mothers* as lesbians who, within their identities as lesbians, had become or were actively seeking (i.e., in the process of adopting or inseminating) to become mothers. Using this definition meant that I was not going to include women who had birthed or adopted children while in heterosexual relationships and later identified as lesbians. I used a more narrow definition because the mothering decisions of lesbians who were originally in heterosexual relationships were likely to involve different factors from those of women who openly identified as lesbians. For example, women in heterosexual relationships have easy access to sperm that can lead to accidental pregnancies. They also face societal pressure, as seemingly heterosexual women, to have children. Because a fundamental component of my study was to understand how sexuality shapes the decision-making process, I only wanted to include women who made mothering decisions within their identities as lesbians.

For childfree lesbians, I wanted to find lesbians who did not want to enter into motherhood and who did not already have children (Bartlett, 1994). I chose the term *childfree* because it does not center *mother* as the norm (as does *nonmother* or *not-mother*) and does not suggest a lack of something (as does *childless* and *nonmother*). To me *childfree* suggested a positive state where women are free from the responsibilities of child-raising (Bartlett, 1994).

Because I wanted a racially and class diverse sample, I also needed to define race and class. As with the term *lesbian,* I asked potential participants to define their own racial identities (Luttrell, 2000). For my focus groups and later my analysis, I collapsed participants into two racial categories: lesbians of color and White lesbians. *Lesbians of color* were those who identified as Black and/or Latina. *White lesbians* were those who identified as Euro-American (i.e., of European descent). I was able to group race into two racial categories without compromising the integrity of the study because my research looked specifically at how racial privilege and discrimination shapes mothering decisions. Therefore, I divided my participants into those who have access to racial privilege (Whites) and those who do not (Blacks and Latinas). Although the census views *Latino* as an ethnicity and not a race, I included Latinas and Blacks in one group because both race and ethnicity are systems of stratification. In addition, ethnicity is related to larger racial categories and cannot be understood outside the history of racial classification in the United States (Barrett and Roediger, 2005; Foley, 2005; Taylor, 2006). To capture the structural and cultural features of racial inequality, sociologists increasingly use the term *racial-ethnic.* In understanding race and ethnicity as they afford or deny White privilege, much of the recent literature contends that Blacks and many groups of Latinos often fall into a similar group in their relationships to White privilege (Bonilla-Silva, 2003; Lipsitz, 2005; Martinez, 2007; R. Smith, 2007). Therefore, to get at a more comprehensive understanding of racial privilege and discrimination, I drew on similar racial-ethnic groupings in my research. As with the category of lesbian, I grouped lesbians based on racial-ethnic self-identification.

Like race, class is a complex social system that can be divided into multiple categories. I decided before recruiting my sample that I would focus on middle-class and working-class lesbians, categories that I initially defined loosely on the basis of education and occupation. Definitions of class also often include income and wealth, but I did not try to determine either of these at the time of recruitment for fear of offending potential participants. Initially I classified working-class participants as those with an associate's degree or less and who worked at "blue-collar" jobs. I classified middle-class participants as those holding a bachelor's degree or higher and who worked at managerial or professional jobs. In cases where education and occupation did not neatly fit into either category, I used any additional information I had about the participants, such as their partner's occupation, to help determine their class position. Because I knew some of the participants through lesbian networks, I often had some additional background information. In cases where I did not have any other information, I asked participants directly for information about their partners and their family background that might help me determine class position.

CHOOSING A METHOD AND RECRUITING A SAMPLE

Once I knew who I was looking for, I then needed to select a method that lent itself to recruiting a diverse group of lesbians who might be difficult to find. I selected focus groups for three main reasons. First, focus groups can reveal a diversity of viewpoints with a small group of people in a relatively short period of time (Jarrett, 1993). Second, focus groups allow homogenous groups of people who have historically had limited power and influence to express their opinions together in a nonthreatening and comfortable setting (Morgan and Krueger, 1993, p. 15). This advantage seemed particularly important when interviewing lesbians of color and working-class lesbians. Third, focus groups are ideal for encouraging participants to discuss in critical ways a topic (such as motherhood) that they may not have really thought about prior to participating in the study (Morgan, 1997; Morgan and Krueger, 1993).

Having decided who I wanted to recruit and how I wanted to interview them, I then needed to figure out how I was going to find them. Before setting off into the field, I made a set of decisions about the geographical area from which I was going to recruit. I chose five counties in a midwestern state because I was familiar with, and had contacts in, those counties. The five counties also offered me access to a large population of lesbians relative to other counties, from which to draw a diversified sample.

After selecting my geographical area, I started identifying and recruiting participants into my study. To do this, I used a variety of strategies. I advertised the study in a publication that reached over two thousand lesbians throughout the state. I spent time in lesbian social locales such as feminist bookstores, coffee houses, and bars. I visited lesbian organizations and religious groups. I advertised at community colleges, four-year colleges, and universities. I also advertised on local online listservs that targeted lesbians of diverse backgrounds. In other words, I contacted and traveled to as many lesbian hangouts as I could find within the five-county area to recruit participants for my study. I visited lesbian social support meetings; I attended lesbian mother support groups; I sat through religious services that were welcoming to lesbians; I contacted community leaders, academics, and factory workers. I spoke with whomever was willing to talk to me about my study.

When I found people who were willing to participate, I did two things. First, I handed them a questionnaire (see appendix A) that provided me with basic contact and demographic information such as occupation, education, individual and household income, and racial-ethnic background. Second, I used a "snowball" sample-recruiting technique, asking lesbians if they knew of anyone else who might be interested in participating in the study. Snowball sampling turned out to be the most effective method of recruitment for my study. As a member of a lesbian mothers' support group and as an active member in the lesbian community, I had access to many White middle-class lesbians, some middle-class lesbians of color, and some White working-class lesbians who fit the criteria for the study. The lesbians I knew in the community helped me make contacts with other lesbians in the area. After contacting the people my initial contacts suggested, I continued to use snowball sampling to expand the sample.

After over four months of recruiting efforts, I had gathered together thirty-five lesbians who were willing to participate in the study. I recruited sixteen (45.7%) participants through snowball sampling, nine (25.7%) from two local lesbian mother groups, six (17.2%) from religious groups or lesbian bars, and the remaining four (12%) from listservs and advertisements/flyers. Twenty-nine (82.9%) of the participants came from my local area (which included a small city with suburban and rural surrounding areas), four (11.4%) came from a large city, and two (5.7%) came from smaller towns in the state.

RECRUITMENT REVELATIONS

Because of all the explaining and traveling and hustling I had to do to find participants, the recruiting of lesbians was the most difficult part of my study. While going through the recruitment process, I had three "recruitment revelations" that led me to understand that recruiting a sample—particularly one that is stratified by race and class—is really hard work. I found that recruiting working-class lesbian mothers, regardless of race, and lesbians of color, regardless of mothering decision, to be particularly difficult. I had hoped to recruit working-class lesbians from a certain county known for its large working-class population. However, despite several contacts I made at colleges, local organizations, and workplaces, I was unable to recruit even one lesbian from that county. Several sources informed me that lesbians in that area are particularly closeted and reluctant to participate in studies. They feared the study would "out" them to family members and co-workers, leaving them facing the loss of jobs and other dire social and economic ramifications. My inability to recruit working-class lesbians from that county was mirrored in other geographical areas. Through all my recruiting efforts I was unable to recruit many working-class mothers of any racial background. As I discuss later in this book, my difficulty in recruiting working-class lesbian mothers was due not only to their fear of having their sexual identities exposed but also to social conditions, such as inflexible work schedules, restricted access to support networks, and the high cost of donor insemination, that limited their opportunities to become mothers.

In addition to the problems of recruiting working-class lesbians, I found there were significant barriers between me and Black lesbian communities. I made numerous unsuccessful trips to recruit lesbians of color from the largest city in the study area. During my recruitment process I learned that Black lesbians were uninterested in my study because many of them had become mothers through previous heterosexual relationships and therefore did not meet a major criterion for participation. Often these women were leaders in their communities. My sense was that because they seemed frustrated by my narrow definition of lesbian mother, they discouraged others from participating in the study. Furthermore, because Black lesbians have experienced discrimination by White lesbians, there was a large racial division in that city's lesbian "community." Because of this, several support groups were only open to lesbians of color. After I spoke with the group leaders, they agreed to allow me to come after the meetings to recruit. The three times I showed up at the end of such group meetings, I discovered that the meetings had been cancelled. Although I did not take these cancellations personally, and while I understand why some meetings are deliberately hidden from White lesbians, the racial divide among lesbians made recruiting very difficult.

My second recruitment revelation was also related to my difficulty in recruiting lesbians of color and working-class lesbians. About halfway through my recruitment efforts it occurred to me what little control I had over the recruitment process. Both feminist and nonfeminist researchers have reflected upon the unequal power structures within researcher-participant relationships. There is no question that researchers have a certain power over participants in that researchers can potentially exploit participants, are often free from the troubles they are studying, and usually have the ultimate say on how to interpret and publish the information they receive from participants (Baca Zinn, 1979; Burawoy, 1991; Gorelick, 1991; Stacey, 1988; Thompson, 1992). Although I agree that there are ethical issues concerning unequal power relations, during the recruitment process I felt as if potential participants had more power over me than I had over them because they had the ability to refuse to participate, thus leaving me without a study. I found this lack of control frustrating, causing me to reflect upon the devastating effects this could have on my research project. This reflection led me to an understanding of how fluid power relations can be within research. During the recruitment process, I might have had power to define terms and include or exclude certain groups of lesbians, but lesbians had similar power over me in that they could chose not to participate in my study. I was frequently reminded of my lack of power over potential participants. In fact, feeling like I was hustling, pestering, and at times nearly begging people to participate was a regular reminder that I was at the mercy of the goodwill of lesbians who might be willing to participate.

My revelation about power relationships led me to my third recruitment revelation and had to do with my own position within the study. As I continued through the recruitment process, I began to recognize myself as a positioned intellectual—as both an insider and outsider—which helped me understand why recruiting at times was easy and at other times extremely frustrating (Andersen, 1993; Baca Zinn, 1979; Gold, 1997; Kennedy and Davis, 1993; Weston, 1991). According to Ohnuki-Tierney (1984) and Lewin (1995b), positioned intellectuals (or what Ohnuki-Tierney refers to as "native anthropologists") are scholars who study their own cultures. Positioned intellectuals may find themselves in the curious position of being "native" (i.e., an insider) to part of their culture, but "foreign" (i.e., an outsider) to other parts.

Having some groups of lesbians perceive me as an insider helped me gain access to those groups. But having some groups perceive me as an outsider made them wary of talking with me and participating in my study. Although I tried to present myself as an insider to all groups of lesbians, my race and class position at times prevented me from being as successful in the recruitment process as I had hoped. In recruiting White lesbians of any class or motherhood status, I was an insider. I knew many of the potential participants, or at least traveled in similar social circles. Even gaining access to groups of White lesbians whom I did not know (e.g., in bars, at church services, or at meetings) involved a comfortable rapport between me and the potential participants. But being a White, middle-class lesbian mother weakened my insider status considerably when trying to recruit lesbians of color, working-class lesbians, and childfree lesbians. I was very much an outsider among many of the groups of lesbians I tried to recruit and often could not gain access to their events and activities. During the few times I did gain access, I felt that the lesbians in the group were keeping their distance from me, being very wary, understandably, of my status as a White lesbian and as a researcher. The result of my insider/outsider status in recruiting was greater access to White middle-class lesbians and a difficulty in recruiting lesbians of color and working-class lesbians. And the more of an outsider I was to any given group of potential participants, the more powerless I felt.

CENTERING LESBIANS' VOICES

Although I faced some constraints in recruiting a diverse sample, by using a combination of sampling strategies and by hustling around five counties for four months, I was able to recruit a fairly diverse sample. In my study there was almost an even division between lesbian mothers (17) and childfree lesbians (18). Participants fell between the ages of 22 and 46 years. Thirteen (37.1%) of the participants were either Black or Latina. The remaining 22 (62.9%) were White. Similarly, I recruited 13 (37.1%) working-class lesbians and 22 (62.9%) middle-class lesbians. As I discuss below, during the focus groups several participants in the middle-class focus group identified themselves as working-class and came from working-class backgrounds. Therefore, the breakdown of participants by class in table 1 is not neatly discernable.

In selecting my sample, I had hoped to recruit at least as diverse a sample as existed in the comparable population of the state in which I conducted my research. That is, I hoped to have a sample that had as least as many women (proportionately speaking) in a given age group who identified as coming from a particular racial-ethnic background as existed in the larger population. In my particular case, to determine whether or not I achieved this goal, I compared the lesbians in my sample (women between the ages of 22 and 46, who identified as White, Black, and Latina/Hispanic) with those in the state population.

Table 2 shows the degree of my success in achieving this goal. The column labeled "Focus Group Participants" represents the percentage of Black and Latina and White lesbians who participated in the study. The column labeled "Comparable State Population" represents the percentage of women between the ages of 22 and 46 living in the research state during 2000, the year I conducted my research, who

TABLE I
Distribution of Participants in Focus Groups

	Working Class	Middle Class	Totals
Black and Latina	5 (14.2%)	8 (22.9%)	13 (37.1%)
White	8 (22.9%)	14 (40.0%)	22 (62.9%)
Totals	13 (37.1%)	22 (62.9%)	35 (100%)

TABLE 2
Racial-Ethnic Stratification in Focus Groups Compared with Women in the State Where the Research Was Conducted, Ages 22–46 (2000)

	Focus Group Participants		Comparable State Population	
Black and Latina	13	(37.1%)	337,443	(19.3%)
White	22	(62.9%)	1,414,508	(80.7%)
Totals	35	(100%)	1,751,951	(100%)

identified themselves as Black, Latina, or White. As Table 2 shows, the percentage of Black and Latina participants in the focus groups (37.1%) is almost double that of Black and Latina women (19.3%) in the research state. In addition, I have a smaller percentage of White women in my sample (62.9%) than in the comparable state population (80.7%).

Table 3 provides some basic information about the 35 participants. They are listed in alphabetical order by name. I have changed the participants' names to protect their identities. The table lists each participant's name, class as I have designated it, racial-ethnic identity as the participant has identified, the participant's mothering desire (i.e., whether she *wanted* to become a mother or to remain childfree), and her mothering decision (i.e., whether she actually *did* become a mother or remain childfree). With the exception of mothering desire, which I determined during the focus groups, I determined all other information during the recruitment process.

CONDUCTING FOCUS GROUPS

Once I grouped my participants by race, class, and mothering decision, I began conducting the focus groups. I held the interviews in places convenient to the participants, particularly at universities, churches, and in their homes. I had a list of open-ended questions that I asked all focus groups (see appendix B and C). During the focus groups, I also allowed the discussions to go in a variety of directions when participants wanted to discuss topics that I had not anticipated. I audiotaped all of the interviews and then transcribed the discussions. Each focus group lasted between two and three hours.

During the interviews I discovered that I had to make some adjustments to the structure of my focus groups. For example, I had decided

TABLE 3
Information about Participants

Name[a]	Age	Class	Race	Mothering Desire	Mothering Decision
Amanda	43	Working	White	Childfree	Childfree
Amy	43	Middle	Black	Childfree	Childfree
Andrea	44	Middle	White	Mother	Childfree
Anita	39	Middle	Latina	Mother	Mother
Barb	46	Middle	White	Mother	Childfree
Beth	45	Middle	Black	Mother	Mother
Carly	38	Middle	White	Unsure	Mother
Clara	33	Working	White	Unsure	Childfree
Desiree	31	Middle	Latina	Mother	Mother
Diane	44	Working	Black	Mother	Undetermined
Eve	31	Working	White	Childfree	Childfree
Grace	30	Middle	White	Mother	Mother
Janet	40	Working	White	Childfree	Mother
Joy	33	Working	Black	Unsure	Childfree
Judy	40	Middle	White	Childfree	Childfree
June	45	Middle	White	Childfree	Mother
Kathy	41	Middle	White	Childfree	Mother
Kerry	32	Working	White	Unsure	Childfree
Kizzy	29	Working	Black	Mother	Undetermined
Kristy	45	Middle	White	Unsure	Childfree
Leslie	36	Middle	Black	Childfree	Childfree
Lily	39	Middle	White	Mother	Mother
Mabel	33	Working	White	Childfree	Childfree
Maria	47	Middle	White	Childfree	Childfree
Martha	22	Working	White	Mother	Mother
Miriam	31	Middle	Black	Childfree	Mother
Pam	46	Middle	Latina	Mother	Childfree
Patricia	45	Middle	White	Unsure	Mother
Rita	42	Middle	White	Mother	Mother
Roxanne	38	Middle	Black	Unsure	Childfree
Sadie	36	Working	White	Mother	Mother
Sara	36	Working	Latina	Unsure	Childfree
Tammy	38	Middle	White	Childfree	Childfree
Tara	34	Middle	White	Unsure	Childfree
Terry	35	Working	Black	Unsure	Childfree

[a] All names have been changed to protect the identity of the participants.

early on not to include intimate partners in the same focus group. If participants had partners who were willing to participate in the study, I originally decided to include the partner in a separate focus group. However, because I had so few lesbians of color and working-class lesbians, on the two occasions when couples showed up unannounced to the focus groups, I let them remain together. Because there is a lack of research discussing the consequences of couples showing up uninvited to focus groups, I can only surmise that this is a hazard of doing research involving same-sex couples. A researcher would be less likely, for example, to have the uninvited spouse of a heterosexual couple show up to a focus group where only husbands or wives were being interviewed. It would be equally unlikely that the researcher would allow the uninvited spouse to stay and participate. Despite this hazard, my experience was that interviewing partners had no negative impact on the study. In fact, because it increased the number of participants, and the participants did not appear to restrict their responses because of the presence of their partners, having both partners present proved to be a positive experience in my study.

In addition, I soon realized that defining class was even more complicated than I had originally anticipated. After the participants filled out an initial demographic questionnaire, I had information about their income, education, and occupation, which I used to determine their class status. However, during the focus groups several participants identified themselves as coming from working-class backgrounds that had clearly shaped their lives in important ways. During my analysis, therefore, I paid close attention to the participants' self-identification of class as well as my own classifications.

FOLLOW-UP INTERVIEWS

In 2006, as I was writing this book, it occurred to me that my research was incomplete. I realized that four of the lesbians whom I interviewed in 2000—Kizzy, Diane, Joy, and Martha—had said they were in the process of becoming mothers, but I did not know if they had achieved this goal. This was particularly important because all four of these participants were working-class, and all but one (Martha) was Black. To draw any conclusions about lesbians' decision-making processes I needed to know the outcome of their mothering desires. In an effort to find out if six years later they had actually become mothers, I set out to ask some follow-up questions.

Finding Martha was relatively easy because I had an old telephone number that led me to a friend of hers who led me to her. Martha was more than willing to answer my questions and informed me that she was currently a foster parent in the adoption process. She was hopeful that the courts would grant her legal custody of her foster child. Joy was a bit more difficult to contact because I did not have updated contact information. However, internet resources being what they are, I was able to find an email address to which she happily responded. Joy told me that after getting a puppy, she had enough responsibility for the time being. She said she would still like to be a mother, but not if it meant parenting without a partner.

Diane and Kizzy, who were partners at the time of the study, were more reluctant to respond than Martha and Joy. Even though I had current contact information and made several attempts to reach them by telephone and email, they did not respond right away. Diane eventually responded, stating that she very much still wanted to become a mother and that her partner was planning on having children. She never stated that she and Kizzy were still together. However, current telephone records indicated that they shared a residence, suggesting that Kizzy was still Diane's partner.

THE FINE PRINT

Although I followed the rules for conducting social science research and recruited and interviewed a diverse group of women, the integrity of my work does not make up for the inherent shortcomings of the research method I used. Because I conducted a qualitative study built on a small sample that was not randomly selected, I cannot generalize my findings to the larger population of lesbians. My study provides important insight into, but not definitive or general information about, groups of lesbians in other geographical locations within the United States. In ethnographic research, the benefit of the methodology lies not in the ability to generalize but in the ability to allow readers to hear the voices of people to whom most readers would not otherwise have access.

The remaining chapters of this book draw on these voices to reveal rich experiences that might otherwise remain hidden. The strength of a feminist methodology is that it brings us to a deeper understanding of women's lives (L. Thompson, 1992). The strength of a multiracial feminist methodology is that it brings us to a deeper understanding of a diverse group of women's lives and creates knowledge that is not obscured by White, middle-class experiences. These strengths are worth all the complexities, frustrations, and even shortcomings inherent in designing and conducting qualitative multiracial feminist research. The voices you will hear in the following chapters draw from my recruitment efforts to illuminate the processes that some lesbians from diverse racial-ethnic and class backgrounds go through to decide to become mothers or remain childfree.

CHAPTER FOUR

Developing Mothering Desires

My original research question focused specifically on how adult lesbians choose to become mothers or remain childfree. However, as I began analyzing the data, it occurred to me that in order to understand how lesbians make their decisions, I needed to better understand how they came to want to become mothers or remain childfree. During the interviews I often heard lesbians state that they "always wanted to become a mother" or they "never wanted to have children." Because mothering desires (i.e., the desires to become mothers or remain childfree) were integral to the identities of many of the lesbians I interviewed, I realized that the development of mothering *desires* is integral to the development of mothering *decisions*. In addition, I found that just as mothering decisions are embedded in social processes, so are mothering desires. The information the women gave me about their childhoods provided insight into a complex process based not on biological urges or socialization but on social experiences and interpretations of those experiences. Like heterosexual women (Gerson, 1985), lesbians in my study did not simply wake up one morning thinking, "I want to be a mother" or "I want to be childfree." The process by which they developed this desire was largely based on the social and cultural conditions in which they grew up.

Because I did not plan on asking lesbians how they developed

their mothering desires, I came upon this information quite unex-
pectedly. In organizing the questions I was going to ask during the
focus groups, a fellow graduate student suggested I start each focus
group with a question that would put participants at ease and gener-
ate wide discussion. Based on this advice, I decided to ask lesbians
how they defined *mother*. I asked what the term meant to them, to
their own mothers, and to the communities in which they grew up.
It was a seemingly simple question, and I expected fairly simple answers like, "A mother is a biological parent who is also a caregiver."
Although I got some such answers, mostly my question sparked a rich
discussion about lesbians' childhood experiences, their relationships
with their own mothers, and reflections on how they negotiated their
sexual identities within their communities and families of origin. In
other words, in answering a seemingly simple question, the lesbians
I interviewed provided the data I needed to understand how they developed early mothering desires. These desires consisted of wanting
to become mothers, wanting to remain childfree, and ambivalence toward motherhood.

Drawing on lesbians' responses, in this chapter I focus on the first
phase of the process of making mothering decisions: *the development
of mothering desires*. Building upon the limited social science research
on early childhood experiences, I found that the processes that lesbians go through involve a combination of four factors: their experiences
as children, how they interpret their own mothers' lives, their early experiences with childcare, and their experiences of racial or gender discrimination. By looking at these factors, my research clearly challenges
the belief that mothering desires are based on biological or hormonal
urges. In fact, my research argues that lesbians' early mothering desires develop out of social conditions. These desires become important
guides for how lesbians negotiate the social and economic barriers
and constraints they face as adults in turning desires into realities.

THINKING ABOUT WOMEN'S DESIRES TO
BECOME MOTHERS

There are three predominant models for thinking about women's
desires to become mothers. Perhaps the most common one is based

on the belief that women want to become mothers because they are biologically programmed to do so. Most people believe that hormones and evolutionary necessity encourage women to want to procreate and give birth. Even the literature on lesbian mothers, which acknowledges that *lesbian mother* has historically been an oxymoron, takes for granted that lesbians, as women, will want to become mothers because their "biological clocks" are ticking (Lewin, 1993).

Sociological research conducted in the 1970s and 1980s began to question this supposed biological mandate by looking at how mothers socialize their daughters toward or away from motherhood. So the second model argues that women develop a mothering desire through socialization. The logic of this model is that mothers teach their daughters that motherhood is either something to aspire to or something to avoid. Despite many people's acceptance of this model, research conducted by Gerson (1985) looking at heterosexual women's mothering desires, what she calls "orientations" toward or away from motherhood, strongly critiques the socialization model. As Gerson (1985) writes:

> Domestic mothers do not necessarily reproduce their own orientation toward mothering and domesticity in their daughters. Nor do nondomestically oriented mothers necessarily produce nondomestically oriented daughters. Although the importance of mothers is undeniable, the *way* in which they are important in shaping their daughters' orientations is complex and open-ended . . . In the long run, daughters must make their own way in the world—informed by, but not controlled by, their mothers' decisions and relationships with them as children. (p. 53)

In other words, although their perceptions of their mothers' lives, as well as other factors, shape girls' thoughts about motherhood, girls are not simply socialized into domestic roles or nondomestic roles by their mothers.

The third model is based on social structural understandings and extends Gerson's challenge of the socialization model. This third model also seriously weakens dominant assumptions about biological mandates and looks at how social and economic factors shape adult women's mothering *decisions* regardless of their mothering *desires*. The research tells us that women's relationship to work, their involvement in intimate relationships, and society's belief that women should be mothers are critical factors in shaping women's mothering decisions. What we know, however, is mostly about women as adults, not as children, and therefore about mothering decisions and not mothering desires. In fact, we know very little about how childhood experiences encourage girls and young women to develop the *desire* to become mothers or remain childfree. What we do know is mostly about middle- and working-class White women (Cain, 2001; Gerson, 1985; Morell, 1994), thus overlooking how structures of sexuality and race might also impact mothering decisions. For heterosexual women, as for the lesbians interviewed in my study, childhood experiences such as mother-daughter dynamics, parental expectations, family dynamics, gender norms, class aspirations, and the wider social environment in which girls grow up help them to develop "orientations" (Gerson, 1985) toward or away from motherhood. However, among heterosexual women, early orientations are poor predictors of adult family patterns (Gerson, 1985). In other words, early childhood experiences help shape girls' *desires* to become mothers or remain childfree, but those desires do not generally tell us whether a heterosexual woman will actually *become* a mother or remain childfree.

My work is closely aligned with the third model. For many of the same reasons as Gerson, my work strongly critiques and challenges biological and socialization models. However, I depart from Gerson, who found that baseline desires are not good predictors of adult decisions. Unlike Gerson, I found that although some lesbians were ambivalent about motherhood, many developed early in their lives strong desires for motherhood or remaining childfree. As I discuss in the following chapters, many lesbians were able to negotiate their lives in ways that allowed them to fulfill their mothering desires. Like heterosexual women (Gerson, 1985), many of the lesbians I interviewed found that additional social conditions, such as work and intimate relationships, pushed them away from their early desires. However, I also found that early mothering desires were much more salient for the lesbians in my study than for the heterosexual women in Gerson's study. I suggest that the reason for this is that even though lesbians' mothering decisions are made through larger social processes and are not as intentional as previous studies have portrayed them to be, they are still more intentional than decisions made by heterosexual women. This is not to say that lesbians have full control over their mothering decisions. However, because lesbians can control whether or not they get pregnant, and because their very identity as lesbians questions dominant gender and sexual ideologies, they have greater control over their mothering decisions than heterosexual women. Therefore, lesbians who have strong desires to become mothers or remain childfree are able to more actively pursue those desires than heterosexual women, even if their desires are challenged later in life.

Despite this greater control over the decision-making process, like Gerson, I too found that it is important to distinguish between the processes lesbians go through to arrive at a mothering *desire* from the social barriers and opportunities that help them *realize* those desires. Just as with heterosexual women, the interplay between the creation of mothering desires and the real opportunities to actualize those desires is key to understanding lesbians' mothering decisions. Much like Gerson, I found that there are two connected phases of the decision-making process: childhood experiences out of which women develop mothering desires, and adult experiences out of which women actually decide to become mothers or remain childfree. I argue that both of these phases develop out of social conditions and that both are important in shaping lesbians' decisions to become mothers or remain childfree. In addition, I question how race and sexuality, in addition to gender and class, shape those social conditions and thus shape the social processes through which lesbians both develop their mothering desires and make their mothering decisions.

HOW LESBIANS INTERPRETED THEIR OWN MOTHERS' LIVES

When I began each focus group by asking participants to discuss their definitions of *mother,* many lesbians, regardless of race, class, or mothering decision, defined a mother as nurturing, providing support and unconditional love, being "there" for her children. For example, Patricia, a middle-class White lesbian, explained with great warmth in her voice:

"[Motherhood is] a pretty big thing, isn't it? It's like everything
from the beginning of the day to the end of the day.

However, some lesbians offered a negative definition. For example,
Kristy, a middle-class White lesbian, defined motherhood as being
"chained" and preventing her from having her own life. Many of these
definitions came out of lesbians' relationships with their own mothers,
as well as their interpretations of their mothers' experiences. Through
their answers, it became clear that how lesbians interpreted their own
mothers' lives played an important role in shaping their own mothering desires.

For the most part, but certainly with exceptions, lesbians with
negative interpretations of motherhood were more inclined to want to
remain childfree, and those with positive interpretations were more
inclined to want to become mothers. However, because interpretations of mothers' lives is not the sole factor shaping mothering desires, and because of social and cultural conditions that women faced
later in life, some lesbians with negative interpretations early on in
life did become mothers as adults, and vice versa. And as studies on
heterosexual women have found (Polatnick, 1996), while ideas about
motherhood as a traditional gender role clearly shaped lesbians' interpretations of motherhood, lesbians' interpretations of motherhood
were also based on complex notions of class and race.

Many of the middle-class lesbians in my study, regardless of race,
interpreted their mothers' lives to be self-sacrificing. Some lesbians,
however, interpreted this sacrifice as a reason to remain childfree,
while others interpreted it to be rewarding and worthwhile, thus leading them to desire motherhood. Among middle-class lesbians of color,
there were two main views. First, some saw motherhood as a self-
sacrifice that is too overwhelming a responsibility to assume. Roxanne, a middle-class Black lesbian, illustrated this point:

I just look at it as I'm just too selfish to do anything like that.
And I don't think of myself as being selfish, just selfish as far
as the responsibilities that come with having a child and having
the ideas that I have about childbearing, being a mother, being
there 24-7, taking the kid here, taking the kid there, all those

things that are built into it. No, no, I can't do that. I don't have
that. I don't think I can do it.

The emphasis by Roxanne and other middle-class lesbians of color on
the ongoing and intense responsibility of motherhood developed, in
part, out of watching their own mothers struggle with raising children. Particularly among Black women, motherhood holds not only
the responsibility of raising and nurturing children but also the historical responsibility of remaining in the work force and "uplifting the
race" to ensure the survival of Black children (Collins, 1990; Silvera,
1995; B. Smith, 1998). The emphasis on motherhood's enormous
responsibility, along with their experiences in watching their own
mothers, led many of the middle-class lesbians of color in my study to
develop a desire for personal freedom that is difficult to achieve when
coupled with mothering responsibilities.

In contrast, however, the second view that some middle-class lesbians of color held was that their mothers' multiple responsibilities were
a welcome challenge that allowed for maternal flexibility. This was
particularly true for lesbians of color who came from single-parent
families. For example, Desiree, a middle-class Latina, stated:

> I was raised by a single parent, and I think she—she never
> married, and it was just—she's very independent. I could never
> imagine her marrying, now or ever, when I was younger or in
> the future. Women could do it. She did everything. She took
> care of everything.

Rather than seeing "doing everything" as a negative condition, Desiree
interpreted her mother's responsibilities as a model for how mothers
can achieve multiple goals. Other middle-class lesbians raised by single mothers had similar experiences. The result was that many lesbians of color from female-headed households were able to accept the
gender roles of motherhood because those gender roles showed them
that motherhood can be flexible rather than restrictive or oppressive to
women. Furthermore, it gave them a model for how women can raise
children outside of marriage. Given that marriage is not an option for
most lesbians in the United States, and certainly not for the lesbians I

interviewed in 2000, this model seemed important in shaping some lesbians' desire for motherhood.

Like their Black and Latina counterparts, middle-class White lesbians also had conflicting interpretations of their mothers' experiences. But their experiences differed slightly because of the structures of race that often privilege White people. Not only did they interpret the self-sacrifices of their mothers' lives as overwhelming, but many middle-class White lesbians also saw their mothers' self-sacrifices as instances of women's oppression. Many discussed how motherhood means staying at home, a position they found to prevent women's personal growth and freedom. As was true for lesbians of color, White lesbians' understanding of motherhood often came from the historical class and race privilege of their mothers. Because middle-class White mothers have often had financial support from husbands that encouraged them not to work, motherhood for middle-class White women has historically meant taking care of children while forgoing higher education and a career (Dill, 1994). I found this also to be true for both White middle-class lesbians who grew up with two parents present and for those whose mothers were divorced or widowed. In this latter group, many lesbians interpreted motherhood as an added burden that forced their mothers into the work force so their families could maintain a middle-class status. As·a result of their race and class status, many White middle-class lesbians saw motherhood as preventing their mothers from finishing their education or pursuing careers of their choice. Tammy explained this point well when she reflected upon her thoughts when she was younger:

> I'm going to [have] a career first, and I'm going to be settled in a career, 'cause . . . I watched my mom raise all these children and not—I mean, she tried to go back to college and wasn't able to do it 'cause there was just too many kids at home. There were four of us and no father, so it was her, and I just thought, "No, that's not going to be me," and then by 30 I thought, "I'm not going to have children."

Based at least partially on her interpretation of her mother's experience as preventing personal freedom in terms of work and educational opportunities, Tammy, like many other middle-class White lesbians, developed a desire to remain childfree. For example, June, a middle-class White lesbian, stated that seeing how her own mother lived and worked led her originally to not want to become a mother herself:

> I had always sworn up and down that I would not be a mother. I didn't want my mother's life. My mother wasn't very happy being at home and being a mother. And so I swore up and down that I didn't want my mother's life.

Despite June's negative interpretations of her mother's life, ultimately she became a mother herself. As I discuss in the following chapters, social conditions, as well as the ability of adult lesbians to renegotiate gendered ideas about motherhood, can change earlier mothering desires into different mothering decisions.

Whereas some lesbians rejected the gender role of stay-at-home mother because they saw it as oppressive, some White middle-class lesbian accepted it. The difference in response is most likely due to interpretations of mothers' lives in combination with other early experiences such as experiences with children. For example, Grace, a middle-class White lesbian, internalized her mother's staying at home as a positive way in which to raise children:

> But my mother was home with us, and I think that that's how I view, that's always how I've always viewed, that I should be home. I've wanted to be home until I was home.

As an adult, Grace put her job as a nurse on hold to take care of her and her partner's son. Her partner's high income allowed Grace to stay at home. After being a stay-at-home mom for two and a half years, Grace was ready to move back into the paid labor force. Her acceptance of her mother's experiences helped shape her own beliefs about mothers as stay-at-home caregivers. However, as she experienced the constraints of this gender role and as her child grew older, she no longer wanted to be a stay-at-home mom but rather wanted to pursue her career as a nurse. Grace combined her acceptance of staying at home with a flexible view of motherhood that some lesbians from similar backgrounds may not have envisioned or may not have been able to realize because of economic obstacles.

Much like Grace, Carly, a middle-class White lesbian, stated that because of her partner's high income and focused career goals, she herself stayed at home:

> We decided that I would stay home and raise the kids and she would work, and so it worked out really well for us because of our ideas about having kids which is that, um—I guess that the way I grew up, I believe that one parent needs to be home with the kids. And since having kids, I've kind of changed that [view]. I would love more than anything to go out and have at least a part-time job. But I love my kids, and I have a hard time thinking about going out and getting a job and not being there for them all the time, you know, so I'm constantly in a battle with that.

Since Carly did not have an established career, a return to the work force seemed more difficult to her than it did to Grace. However, her partners' financial stability, coupled with her acceptance of the gender role that mothers stay at home, allowed her to fulfill her desire to be a stay-at-home mother.

Just as middle-class lesbians of different racial backgrounds developed distinct interpretations of their mothers' lives, so did working-class lesbians. In addition to focusing on self-sacrifice, oppression, flexibility, and the value of staying at home, working-class lesbians talked about trying to achieve upward mobility and independence. The theme of upward mobility and achieving higher economic status than their mothers was most greatly shared among working-class lesbians of color. For example, Pam, a Latina from a working-class background, stated that having children was not just a personal burden on her mother but a financial burden on her family:

> There are seven children in my family, and my mother made a lot of sacrifices for us. She stayed at home. My father's Hispanic. He didn't want my mother to work. At that time, you know, motherhood seemed like it was just a burden. I mean,

having a lot of children but not a lot of money and seeing
what sacrifices my parents had, [I] reasoned I didn't want to
be responsible for a child as someone who didn't have a lot
of money.

Pam attributes her mother's position to her father's racial-ethnic beliefs about gender roles in families. Although it is unlikely that women
in a lesbian household would experience such strict gender roles (Sullivan, 1996), Pam's desire for upward mobility for herself and her potential children, coupled with the "burden" of motherhood, contributed to her lifelong ambivalence about whether to have children.

White working-class lesbians offered similar interpretations, explaining that their mothers' struggle to support and keep their families together taught them to be independent and strong. Working-class
White mothers lead difficult lives, working long hours both in and
outside the home. Unlike middle-class parents, working-class parents have less quality time for themselves and face more uncertainty
about their children's futures (Rubin, 1992). In my study, working-
class White lesbians reported that their mothers taught them to be
strong and independent, so as to achieve greater personal freedom
and higher economic status. For example, Mabel stated:

My mom raised us different than she was raised. She wanted
us to be strong and wanted us to be independent at a young age
because she was so naive. When she was growing up she went
from her mother's home to her husband's home and never really learned how to be her own person. She was a mom before
she was even an adult, and I think she really just didn't want
that to happen again to her children. So she went kind of the
opposite direction, and maybe a little too strong, to make sure
that we were independent and weren't naive or didn't get taken
advantage of, maybe, the way she felt she did.

The combination of not wanting to struggle economically as their
mothers did, and having been taught to be independent and strong so
they could avoid economic hardship, helped some working-class lesbians develop a desire for personal and economic freedom that contributed to their desire to remain childfree.

EXPERIENCES AS CHILDREN

In addition to their interpretations of their own mothers' lives, lesbians' past family experiences were important in shaping their desires to become mothers or remain childfree. These family experiences varied by race and class. Middle-class lesbians of color did not discuss their family experiences in any detail. In contrast, working-class lesbians of color discussed positive family experiences that contributed to a positive view of motherhood and of family in general. For example, Diane, a working-class Black lesbian, stated:

> I just always wanted . . . I wanted what everyone else had. For
> years I wanted . . . I mean, I actually said it: I wanted a house,
> I wanted a white fence, I wanted kids and a dog and the whole
> family thing. I think for me it has to do with my childhood. I
> want to relive [my] childhood with my child. And that's fun.
> There's a lot of enjoyment.

For Diane, the experience of being raised by a single mother helped instill a positive view of motherhood and family that led her to desire motherhood.

Kizzy, also a working-class Black lesbian, echoed Diane's desire to recreate her childhood experiences. However, Kizzy explained this desire as it relates to an extended Black family and sense of community:

> KIZZY: I know some of the parts where people get raised by
> their grandmothers, by their aunts, by different people. I
> think that's pretty widespread as far as I've seen in the Black
> community, because, I mean, it's just normal. I mean, the
> person might not even be related to you. You have things
> where you say, "So and so is my play mother or my play
> brother or play sister." So there's this idea that it's not just
> blood that can tie people together. But you can decide who
> you want to be your family, and take them in that way.

> DIANE: I agree with Kizzy as far as the Black community. For
> years it's been the family raising you. It's not just your par-
> ents. Your uncle will come in, and people on the street. If

> as a child I was seen throwing rocks at a window and Betty
> Johnson that lives down the street, she would be on the
> phone calling my mother to tell me, "Did you know your
> daughter . . . ?" So it's a group effort to raise the children. It
> was. It's not anymore.

This discussion illustrates three themes found in the literature on Black families. First, Kizzy's description of the flexible definition of mother within Black families helps Black lesbians form positive views of motherhood. Previous literature supports this finding that Black communities have flexible and broad definitions of mother (Collins, 1990). Second, Kizzy's definition of mother shows that as a member of a Black community, she has learned that families do not simply consist of biological ties. Rather, the notions of "play family" or "fictive kin" (Dill, 1994) allow her as a lesbian to construct a flexibly defined family of choice (Weston, 1991). Third, Diane's response shows her sense of the strong connection between family and community. She views that connection as a positive influence on children, one that she would like to maintain in her adult life. The powerful connection between family and community is a common theme among Black families (hooks, 1989), and this connection strongly shaped Kizzy's and Diane's desires to become mothers.

White lesbians also discussed family experiences. However, unlike working-class lesbians of color who wanted to recreate positive family experiences, negative family experiences led White lesbians, regardless of class, to desire motherhood. Perhaps in an effort to compensate for negative childhood experiences, White lesbians wanted to transform those experiences into a positive view of what mothers can and "ought" to be. That is, negative family experiences created an emotional void that some White lesbians wanted to fill by becoming mothers. For example, Carly, a middle-class White lesbian, stated that she wanted to mother in order to right the wrongs of her childhood:

> In my family there was—they just had kids, you know. And it
> wasn't that they loved us or they wanted us around or anything.
> When I was growing up, it was kids were seen and not heard.
> And I wanted six kids just so that I could treat them differently.

By mothering her two children in a more loving manner than she herself had experienced, Carly was able to live up to her idea of the mother as nurturer and at least partially make up for past family experiences.

Similarly, Martha, a working-class White lesbian, made it clear that her negative family experience while growing up shaped her beliefs about motherhood and her decision to fill a void from her childhood. Her birth mother was a drug addict, and she was put up for adoption when she was young. Although she was not particularly close to her adoptive siblings, she had a good relationship with her adoptive mother, which may also have shaped her desire to become a mother.

Lesbians' experiences as children clearly influenced their mothering desires. Although middle-class lesbians of color were largely silent on this topic, working-class lesbians of color expressed the desire to recreate positive childhood experiences and become mothers. In contrast, the working-class White lesbians I interviewed spoke of negative childhood experiences that motivated them to create their own families through which to create positive experiences. As the above reflections illustrate, lesbians form beliefs and values about motherhood out of real experiences.

EARLY EXPERIENCES WITH CHILDCARE

Another important childhood experience that shaped lesbians' mothering desires was their experiences with children. Many of the lesbians who discussed past experiences with children were inclined to remain childfree. Several of the lesbians I interviewed helped raise children in some capacity, particularly when they came from large families. In many cases their experiences led them to understand the responsibility of childrearing as a burden.

While there is some variation by race with respect to past experiences with children, there are more notable variations by class. Working-class lesbians were more likely to have taken care of younger siblings, family members' children, or their partners' children. In my study, working-class White lesbians at times found themselves in parental roles because of family emergencies. This was true for both Kerry and Sadie. Kerry and her partner served as temporary mothers to Kerry's niece and two nephews for several years after the children's parents separated and could no longer take care of the children. However, Kerry's experience ended with the parents taking the children back. In Sadie's case, the emergency foster care she provided turned into a permanent situation:

> It was a distant relative, so it was a protective services case. I wasn't a foster parent—nothing. And [child protective services] just called me up one day. I was on my way out to work, and they were like, "Take these kids. We're taking them out of the house." So I kind of had a panic attack, freaked out, and thought, "Oh my God! How can I do this? I can't be a mother and I can't be a parent." That was a year and a half going on two years ago. And now I wouldn't trade [them] for the world. There's nothing like it . . . One will be 6 in the fall, and Caitlin is the youngest. She will be 2 in August. And they're actually legally considered foster children at this point. They're in the process of doing the termination and all that kind of thing, and then I plan to adopt if everything goes right, knock on wood.

In both cases, had Kerry and Sadie not taken the children, the larger family problems would have led to the children being placed in foster care. Their experiences most likely came out of the lack of financial support and stability that many working-class families face. Issues of economic instability as well as the inability to afford outside childcare leads working-class families to rely on family members for daily childcare responsibilities and can also lead to family breakdowns that require other family members to step in as "temporary mothers" (Newman, 1988; Rubin, 1992).

In addition to lesbians' experiences taking care of relatives' children on an extended basis, other working-class lesbians, regardless of race, often had the experience of caring for younger siblings or their partners' children. Terry, a working-class lesbian of color, discussed two experiences with children that shaped her desire to remain childfree:

> Basically my decision was based on family. I grew up in a big family, and I guess, you know, everything had to be shared.

And you learned how to get along with everybody that's in the family itself, but once you get your little freedom, you want to keep it that way. Which is very true. I come from a family of seven children, so I think that was enough. And I've had a few partners, well, a couple of partners, that had children, and I love kids, so I mean that's never been a problem. But I had one incident [when I had] to discipline the child, and I was like, "Okay, no more dealing with other people's children, either."

Terry's statement shows that her experience with her younger siblings and with her previous partners' children affected her desire, and ultimately her decision, to remain childfree.

For working-class participants, the experience of caring for younger siblings was also coupled at times with gender roles that some lesbians found undesirable. For example, Sara, a working-class Latina, explained that her desire to remain childfree developed out of a combination of past experiences with children and a rebellion against the gender roles she experienced in a household with a strongly gender-based division of labor:

You know, for me, I can remember as far back in my life saying, "I'm not having kids." And I think it could have a lot to do with having so many siblings and being the only girl. You're depended upon a little bit more than the boys. And my father's Mexican, and he comes from a very traditional family lifestyle, and my mother [had] a very traditional role as a mother and a housekeeper, so I was expected to follow her path. I've been told you have to learn how to sew and you have to learn how to cook so you can take care of your family and take care of your husband, and then having to do that for my brothers. From the get-go I said I wouldn't have kids. You know, I just wouldn't have them.

Sara's reflections illustrate how for some lesbians, past experiences with children are based on structures of gender that create certain expectations for females. These experiences create a view of motherhood as oppressive, a view that led Sara and other lesbians to want to remain childfree.

While working-class lesbians primarily had past experiences with their partners' children, younger siblings, or the children of other relatives, middle-class lesbians tended to have experiences with their partners' children and unrelated children. For example, Judy, a middle-class White lesbian, described how her past experience as a camp counselor shaped her desire to remain childfree:

> I grew up in [the] camp systems, and the trip systems and doing stuff with the counselors and things. And what we were doing was working with children during the summer . . . We used to joke that it took us two weeks to undo what it took the parents however many years to do, to get them to play in the mud and the rain and things like that. But from that experience I think I got my concept that I didn't want to be a parent. It was too much work, and there were too many strange things that could go wrong.

Judy's comment shows how past experiences with children bring attention to the work involved in raising children and to the potential problems that can arise.

Although class structures created some variations in lesbians' experiences with children, the end result was the same: past experiences with children gave lesbians insight into the responsibilities of having children. This insight helped lesbians of all classes and races formulate views of motherhood as carrying too much responsibility, being too risky (in terms of what can go wrong), or being too embedded in oppressive gender roles. Those who had negative experiences with children began to reject motherhood early on and to develop a desire for personal freedom. Clearly not all lesbians have negative experiences with children. However, the positive experiences did not seem significant enough to warrant discussion during the focus groups. In my study, it was the negative experiences that weighed most heavily on lesbians' minds.

RACIAL AND GENDER DISCRIMINATION

One of the most disturbing experiences that shaped lesbians' mothering desires was the intersection of racial and gender discrimination.

Middle-class lesbians of color in particular focused on the impact of race discrimination on their desires to remain childfree. Many of the middle-class Black participants stated that the racial discrimination they faced as children or young adults was a major factor that deterred them from wanting children. Roxanne stated this point most force-fully and also discussed how for women of color, racial discrimination is coupled with gender discrimination:

> It's just like a reality to me not to want to give birth to a child for color reasons . . . I would not want [my child to] go through what I know what I went through as a Black female. I would not do that to my child. If I could not encapsulate it away from the way I felt from being a Black female, I can't do that. That's not the reality of it. So I choose not to [become a mother] just be-cause of those reasons. That right there. I don't know if Amy or Leslie ever think about that or ever thought about that, I don't know, as being other Black females. I have no idea. That was, we were encapsulated in this Black family and now to know that people could be so cruel to you just because of color.

Both Leslie and Amy agreed with Roxanne. Amy said that she did not experience racial discrimination until she left her parents' house and was in college. Like Roxanne, she emphasized that you cannot prepare a child for such cruelty.

Interestingly, working-class lesbians of color did not discuss racial discrimination as a reason for wanting to remain childfree. There are several possible explanations for this class discrepancy. First, I only interviewed five working-class lesbians of color, one of whom (Sara) was a light-skinned Latina. Second, the working-class lesbians may have grown up in racially segregated communities that shielded them from daily interactions with Whites. On the other hand, middle-class Blacks may have been somewhat integrated into White communities, thus exposing them to more White interaction and discrimination. Third, class and financial issues may have been more salient than race for the working-class group. As Terry stated, "You know, I want to be financially stable, that's number one." Among middle-class lesbians of color, only Pam (who came from a working-class background) mentioned money as being a salient concern. Race might stand out more clearly than class to middle-class lesbians because they are privileged by class. Rather than reporting racial discrimination as the cause of their concerns about motherhood, working-class lesbians of color reported financial issues as their biggest concerns. As I discuss in the following chapter, discrimination along lines of race, class, gender, and sexuality remained an important factor in determining whether or not lesbians actually became mothers. But racial discrimination loomed large in the minds of many women who experienced the harsh realities of racism and sexism during their girlhood years when they were forming their mothering desires.

BEYOND BIOLOGY AND SOCIALIZATION

What is interesting about how lesbians developed their mothering desires is that they drew on personal experiences, the interpretation of those experiences, and larger social relations that shaped personal experiences, to develop their desires to become mothers or remain childfree. In particular, how lesbians interpreted their mothers' experiences, their experiences as children, their experiences with children, and race and gender discrimination all intertwined to shape how lesbians developed their mothering desires. These conditions at times intertwined in ways that left some lesbians ambivalent, not really knowing how they saw themselves in relation to motherhood. But more often than not, these experiences left lesbians with a sense of whether they wanted to become mothers or remain childfree. As table 3 in chapter 3 shows, twelve lesbians in the study wanted to remain childfree, thirteen wanted to become mothers, and ten were ambivalent.

My findings support literature on heterosexual women that challenges the idea that girls develop mothering desires simply on the basis of how their parents socialized them. I found that although mothers do socialize their daughters and that socialization does have an impact, it is not simply socialization but rather an array of additional social and economic factors—such as interpretations of their mothers' experiences, their own childhood experiences, and discrimination—that shape lesbians' development of mothering desires. In addition, the factors that shape lesbians' mothering desires are themselves shaped by larger structures of race, class, and gender.

Furthermore, as this chapter demonstrates, what goes into the desire to become a mother or remain childfree is far more complicated than mere biology. Rather than focusing on biological clocks, hormones, or other biological determinants, the lesbians in my study discussed components of social decision-making processes that strongly shaped their mothering desires. In fact, biological theories offer little if any explanation for why women choose *not* to have children. It is only when we look at the social context within which women grow up, and then later live as adults, that we can truly understand the reasons behind women's mothering decisions.

This chapter highlights how girls' experiences, and their interpretations of those experiences, shape lesbians' mothering desires. Their desires do not form simply out of biological urges or the transmission of domestic values through parental socialization. Rather, their mothering desires develop out of a complex interaction of experiences and interpretations of those experiences. And those experiences are shaped by gender, race, and class structures that guide society's beliefs about what girls, women, and people of color should, and can, do. Those experiences are also based on the real opportunities and constraints built into class structures, whereby some families have more access to resources than other families. While this chapter focused on the development of lesbians' mothering desires, the following chapters will explain how lesbians consider four different factors that ultimately turn their mothering desires into mothering decisions.

CHAPTER FIVE

Understanding Motherhood

It is one thing to desire something; it is quite another to achieve it. As Gerson (1985) found with heterosexual women, and as I found with lesbians, mothering desires do not neatly determine mothering decisions. Regardless of what the lesbians in my study wanted in terms of motherhood or remaining childfree, as they moved through adult lives, there were four main factors—beliefs about motherhood, access to lesbian support networks, intimate partners, and work—that they weighed in ultimately converting their mothering desires into mothering decisions. This chapter discusses the first of these factors.

Although the lesbians in my study developed their mothering desires as children, on the basis of girlhood beliefs about what motherhood was or ought to be, the experiences they had as adults often led them to question, challenge, and sometimes transform those beliefs. For some of the lesbians I interviewed, their beliefs about gender roles created psychological barriers against motherhood that contributed to their decisions to remain childfree. These lesbians often rejected the idea of getting pregnant or adopting children, therefore eliminating their major options for becoming mothers. Many of them also held negative views of lesbian motherhood, further encouraging them to remain childfree. Still others revisited and renegotiated their early beliefs about gender and sexuality such that they developed positive views of lesbian motherhood and therefore could envision becoming mothers. Whatever their personal views, these lesbians balanced dominant understandings of motherhood with their own beliefs and experiences to make their mothering decisions.

Beliefs about motherhood cover a broad range of ideas that vary depending on race, class, gender, and sexuality. For White women, the process of identifying oneself as a mother or childfree woman is shaped by specific class positions. Working-class White women identify themselves as adults through the process of having a child and becoming a mother. In contrast, middle-class White women feel they gain maturity through other identities, such as work and marriage prior to having a child. How White women identify themselves as adults affects not only when they will have children but if they will have them at all (McMahon, 1995).

Beliefs about motherhood also differ by race. For Black women, motherhood extends beyond the White definition of biological mother to include "othermothers" (Collins, 1990; Greene, 1998). Such mothers may be grandmothers, sisters, aunts, cousins, or close friends who take on childcare responsibilities for one another's children (Collins, 1990). Othermothers can also be political advocates who nurture the Black community as a whole (Collins, 1990; Polatnick, 1996). In addition, while middle-class White women in the 1960s and 1970s came to understand motherhood to be a source of oppression because it prevented them from entering the labor force and attaining higher education (Polatnick, 1996), motherhood for Black women often invokes a sense of power. Black women see themselves as the "lifeline" of the Black community, their roles as mothers being a way of "uplifting the race" and maintaining the physical and emotional survival of their children (Collins, 1990; Silvera, 1995; Smith, 1998). Perhaps because of this, larger African-American communities often perceive Black lesbians as cutting the community's "lifeline" and threatening the continuation of the group (Clarke, 1983; hooks, 1989; Silvera 1995).

Black women are also often raised to be strong and independent; therefore, marriage is not a prerequisite for motherhood (Blum and Deussen, 1996; Jarrett, 1994). This belief developed out of Black women's historical and continuing relationship between motherhood and work, whereby Black women have been forced into working for a wage in order to sustain their families. A possible assumption might follow that Black women's independence from men and motherhood outside of marriage would pave a potential path for Black lesbians wanting to raise children because "out" lesbians are at least sexually independent from, and do not generally get married to, men. However, because of homophobia within Black communities (see chap. 2), this assumption is largely false.

As with Whites and Blacks, historical and current race and class relations shape Latino beliefs about motherhood. However, because groups of people labeled "Latino" or "Hispanic" are so diverse, generalizing along racial-ethnic lines is difficult (Clarke, 1983; Espín, 1997; Morales, 1990). Looking specifically at Chicano/a (e.g., Mexican-American) families points to specific beliefs about motherhood. While Chicano/as see motherhood and household chores as a primary responsibility and role of women, Chicanas often work as both mothers and paid laborers (Baca Zinn, 1979; Segura, 1994; Segura and Pierce, 1993). Because of extended kin networks, working mothers often rely on family childcare rather than institutional care. In some working-class families where women work and men's schedules permit, fathers take on major childcare responsibilities (Lamphere, Zavella, and Gonzalez, 1993; Segura, 1994; Zavella, 1987). Because of economic constraints, therefore, women and men in Chicano/a families may alter traditional beliefs about gender roles to accommodate economic realities (Segura, 1994).

In addition, like Black women, Chicanas often see motherhood as a cooperative endeavor wherein other women help mothers with childcare (Segura and Pierce, 1993). The implication of this type of mothering is that Chicano children grow up with multiple mother figures. This not only presents the idea that children can be raised by multiple women, but it also exposes them to a greater range of "gender-related cultural behaviors" and role models (Segura and Pierce, 1994, p. 76).

Examining beliefs about motherhood raises questions about how lesbians from diverse race and class backgrounds internalize and negotiate differing beliefs about motherhood. It also invites us to ask how that internalization and negotiation affects lesbians' mothering decisions. Drawing on the voices of the lesbians I interviewed, this chapter answers these questions.

REJECTING PREGNANCY AND ADOPTION

An important belief that shaped lesbians' mothering decisions focused on pregnancy and adoption. Although I did not ask any specific questions during the focus groups about pregnancy or adoption, throughout the interviews many lesbians, particularly those who wanted to remain childfree, discussed why they did not want to get pregnant or adopt children. Having an aversion to one or the other or both, these lesbians greatly limited their options for becoming mothers. Although their reasons varied by race and class, lesbians generally rejected pregnancy and/or adoption because they never wanted to get pregnant and had not seriously considered adoption. Like White heterosexual women (Bartlett, 1994; Veevers, 1980), many White lesbians, regardless of class, stated that they never wanted to get pregnant. This did not mean, however, that they were necessarily averse to becoming mothers. Rather, they did not want to be the ones to carry the child. For example, Barb, a middle-class White lesbian, would have co-parented if she had found a partner who wanted to get pregnant or adopt. Barb wanted to become a mother but stated, "I would never be the biological mother, never desired that."

Whereas those who did not want to get pregnant were mostly White, those who were not interested in adoption tended to be working-class lesbians of color. When I asked whether or not they had considered adoption, both Terry, a working-class Black, and Sara, a working-class Latina, said no:

TERRY: No, I never thought of adopting. Not at all.

NM: Why not?

TERRY: Um, hmm, mainly because I don't know what type of—you know, they can give you background information on the children prior to you adopting them, but I don't know. That's just never, never dawned on me, I guess. I never thought about it, so I don't think I would. I'm not in that situation as to where I want to be a parent right now, or to be a parent real bad, you know?

SARA: Not too much. I haven't given it a lot of thought because it's not—I've never really had the desire to have a child. I've tossed the idea around. I don't know if I would be in favor of bringing a child into my household through adoption, just because if I were to make that commitment I think I would want it to come from my lineage and my background. Between that with kids sometimes, depending on what they've gone through and what age they're at when they go through the adoption, sometimes it might be even added responsibility if they've got other things that they have to deal with, you know? You could be in store for something you don't even know at the time of adoption that you'll have to deal with. So I'd rather, if I'm going to do it, know what I'm going to get into just from my background and where I'm coming from.

In addition to not having any urge to get pregnant and not thinking of adopting, lesbians who wanted to remain childfree, regardless of race or class, cited a number of reasons for rejecting pregnancy, including personal aversions, physical barriers, and economic expenses. Many lesbians stated that they did not want to go through the hassle of being pregnant for nine months or the pain of labor and delivery. Much like childfree heterosexual women (Bartlett, 1994; Veevers, 1980), lesbians' understanding of pregnancy, labor, and delivery led to an aversion to pregnancy and childbirth. As Amanda, a working-class White lesbian, explained, some of these feelings developed out of watching a friend or family member go through labor and delivery:

The nine-month pregnancy and the delivery. I actually saw my last niece born, and I cannot understand how anybody would go through that.

Rejecting pregnancy because it was an undesirable and painful process supported the view held by many lesbians who wanted to remain childfree: motherhood is undesirable for multiple reasons.

Some lesbians also stated they would not get pregnant because of the physical barriers same-sex relationships present. The very nature of same-sex relationships prevents accidental pregnancies from occurring, and many lesbians were not willing to intentionally try to get pregnant. Lesbians discussed how because of this, choosing to remain childfree was easier for them than for heterosexual women. Sara, a working-class Latina, stated:

> Biologically, I think, well, I have a couple of good [heterosexual] friends that got pregnant by accident. And because of same-sex sex, you don't have that worry. I have good friends that were forced into parenthood because abortion was not an avenue for them. So their marriages didn't work out, and they became mothers because they were in relationships and they ended up getting pregnant even though it wasn't planned. Because lesbians generally do not have sexual intercourse with men, they have very little chance of getting pregnant by accident.

By focusing on accidental pregnancies among heterosexual women, Sara's comment highlights the intentional nature of lesbians' decisions. It also shows how some lesbians view the "plight" of heterosexual women being saddled not only with a child they did not plan on having but with a ruined marriage and single motherhood. Given this view of motherhood in general, and the lack of accidental pregnancies among lesbians, it is not surprising that some lesbians chose to remain childfree.

Lesbians also rejected pregnancy and adoption because both cost so much money. Even middle-class lesbians commented on cost, particularly those who saw children as detracting from their ability to raise or maintain their class status. As I discuss in chapter 8, lesbians understood the high cost of conceptive technologies and their ability, or inability, to afford them. This was particularly true for working-class lesbians in the study, who also lacked health benefits from their jobs that might help offset some expenses incurred through donor insemination. Kristy, a middle-class White lesbian who came from a working-class background, commented:

It costs money to get pregnant in the first place that it doesn't cost straight people. Or adoption, of course, costs money. I just finished reading a book by a gay father who wrote about what he and his partner went through and the amount of money they had to pay to adopt a child. And my jaw just dropped. I mean, I couldn't imagine having $15,000 laying around that I could afford to spend just to get a child. And then on top of that . . . feeding it, raising it, and sending it to college. I think that puts child-rearing out of a lot of people's reach in that way.

Kristy's concerns about the cost of pregnancy, adoption, and child rearing in general were echoed by other lesbians, particularly those from working-class backgrounds. Because one of Kristy's goals was to maintain her middle-class status, laying out money for donor insemination or adoption was not a desirable option for her.

While some lesbians rejected pregnancy or adoption because they thought both were too physically, emotionally, and financially painful, Roxanne, a middle-class Black lesbian, stated that a combination of factors, including her own beliefs about motherhood and sexuality, led her to reject pregnancy. Roxanne not only thought pregnancy was too painful, but she also believed that women should only get pregnant through heterosexual intercourse:

I'm still in the mindset of heterosexual birthing. I haven't gotten to the point of going to a clinic or any of the other stuff. I'm still in the same old natural way of having babies, so therefore I can't go—I don't know that side.

Even though Roxanne ultimately decided not to get pregnant, making that decision was difficult for her. Pressure from, and a desire to please, her mother encouraged her to consider pregnancy and motherhood:

My mother—I mean, you know, it's your mother. My mother gave me everything that she thought you should have. She gave it to you, whatever it was. And it's taken years for me to become strong with my viewpoint, strong with my opinion, and it has gotten me through some worried moments where I might have dipped in the pool to heterosexuality thinking, "Oh, maybe let me see if I can ... "

Although Roxanne was the only one in my study who voiced the opinion that pregnancy should be reserved for heterosexual women, her comment is important because it presents the possibility that other lesbians outside my study share her viewpoint. Roxanne's discussions throughout the interview also suggest that she struggled with a combination of racial discrimination, traditional gender roles, and the omnipresent heterosexism that existed in her family and communities of origin. In her case, the intersections of race, class, gender, and sexuality clearly shaped her decision to remain childfree.

NEGATIVE UNDERSTANDINGS OF LESBIAN MOTHERHOOD

Roxanne's statement also suggests that lesbians have mixed feelings about lesbian motherhood. During the interviews, some lesbians who desired to remain childfree, as well as those who were ambivalent about motherhood, voiced skepticism about lesbian motherhood. Their skepticism came out of their combined understandings of motherhood, sexuality, and gender roles. Because the literature on lesbian mothers focuses on whether or not lesbians are transforming, or assimilating into, the heterosexual institution of motherhood, I asked lesbians for their opinions on this debate. The answers they provided showed a wide breadth of responses and offered insight into what the women in my study thought about lesbian motherhood in general. Their critique came from the belief that lesbians are entering into motherhood to gain heterosexual privilege without thinking seriously enough about the responsibilities involved. For example, Roxanne, a middle-class Black lesbian, stated:

ROXANNE: Overall, as far as becoming a mother, I think it's something that's very serious, and if you choose to do that I think, you know, there should be questionnaires filled out because not everybody might have the "mother, nurturing" aspect of it all. And just because you think you should have a child for your connection with the heterosexual world or

it's a new fad, I still think that the title of mother and how I
see it is just great, and I don't think it should ever be taken
lightly.

NM: Do you think that lesbians who are getting pregnant or
adopting children are taking it lightly?

ROXANNE: Yes.

NM: In what way?

ROXANNE: 'Cause it's just not—it's more to it. It's a big responsibility. I mean, even with the gender of your child and the
society that we live in, it's almost like Pam said, "selfish." I
always thought it was selfish for me to not have one. But to
me it's selfish for you to encapsulate that into your sexuality.
It's a big entity. Being a mother is very important, and to do
that, just—I don't. No, I don't. I can't explain it.

Roxanne's sentiment that lesbians are entering into motherhood
to gain heterosexual privilege without fully considering the consequences and responsibilities was shared by other childfree lesbians in
my study, regardless of race and class.

In addition to gaining heterosexual privilege, some lesbians questioned the idealistic beliefs surrounding lesbian motherhood and believed that ultimately lesbian mothers are really just like heterosexual
mothers. This critique came up during the interviews, and also from
a growing body of literature, suggesting that lesbians create equal
partnerships because their relationships are not dictated by historical
gender-based divisions of labor (Lewin, 1994; Sullivan, 1996). To illustrate this point, Amanda, a working-class White lesbian, stated:

I know that [my] friends who were trying [to get pregnant]
had all wonderful great philosophies about how everything's
reached by consensus, you know, all the lesbian rhetoric that
we, us older ones, maybe have heard when we were coming out
and stuff, you know, all the great utopia that we were developing with the women's land and that. But when it comes to eight
o'clock in the morning and the kid isn't on the bus yet, when

it comes to spilled milk all over the cereal table, or put their clothes on backward, or something like that, or on this morning they wouldn't put their clothes on at all, I think that you're gonna just come back to the very basics. "Get those clothes on now," you know. And you've got a short temper, you're trying to hurry. It's just, it's gonna be the same as it always has been. I think that the philosophy and the idealism is great, and if in the moments of peace and quiet can instill that in your children that everybody is the same and everybody's differences are okay and all of this is wonderful. But like I said, when it comes right down to that moment and you're trying to get into the car and the kids are not cooperating, you're the same as the heterosexual sisters.

Similarly, other lesbians I interviewed did not think lesbian motherhood was so unique or different from heterosexual motherhood. One reason for this was that the lesbians they saw having children were middle-class and doing many of the same things as middle-class heterosexual mothers. For example, Judy, a middle-class White lesbian, stated:

I don't see the people that I know that are having children raising their children any different than I see heterosexual people raising their children now. I think the wild differences in parenting happened a while ago. They happened in the '60s. That's where you got the differences in how people were raising their kids, and the kind of environment that they put their kids in. But that's old, that's passé. We're into yuppies now. Most of the people I know are baby-boomer people having children, and I don't see them being any different in what they do with their children . . . They're taking them to soccer, driving them everywhere under the sun, taking them to Disney World a hundred times, and all this other stuff . . . Oh, they overwhelm the children with stuff.

Although Judy did not specifically acknowledge the middle-class privilege of the lesbians she saw raising children, her use of the word *yuppies* (an acronym for "young urban professionals"), as well as her description of the activities she saw them engaging in, suggests middle-class status.

Judy was not alone in her analysis of how middle-class lesbians are not just assimilating into heterosexual motherhood but are also assuming the privileged trappings of middle-class motherhood. Pam, a Latina from a working-class background, who struggled greatly with her decision to remain childfree partially because of financial constraints, stated:

> I've seen couples who have had children. They emulate the way
> that they were brought up or the class that they were brought
> [up] in. I don't think that we talk enough about class issues in
> this country, but there are definite classes. And I kind of grew
> up in like working-class and of course we aspired to be middle-
> class. And so I see a lot of the women that I know who have
> had children came from middle-class. They, you know, they get
> their houses and they want their children to go to a good school
> and things like that; just the kinds of middle-class values and
> issues that happen. Those are the things that those women are
> coping with, and they're the women who could afford to make
> the choice to have children.

Pam's ideas about lesbian motherhood reinforced her own class reality, leading her to the understanding that lesbian motherhood is something only financially stable middle-class lesbians can achieve. Her own lack of class privilege, therefore, deterred her from having children.

In addition to holding ideological and class-based views against lesbian motherhood, another factor that led some lesbians to have negative understandings of lesbian motherhood was sexual discrimination. Stemming from systems of compulsory heterosexism, many of the lesbians I interviewed had experienced some form of sexual discrimination, or a negative reaction to their sexual identities, in different social arenas, including their families of origin, communities, work, and the medical and legal systems. Sexual discrimination stems from a lack of legal protection against discrimination leveled at people

of diverse sexualities. Such discrimination puts lesbians at risk of losing their jobs, their housing, their health benefits, their legal rights to
inheritance and children, among other things, simply because they
are lesbians. Heterosexist policies support the homophobic ideology
that allows heterosexual people to feel justified in calling lesbians
names, committing acts of violence against them, and generally dis-
criminating against them on a very personal level.

I found that some lesbians internalized sexual discrimination such
that they held negative feelings about themselves, feelings that encouraged them to remain childfree. Although most lesbians in my
study, regardless of race and class, mentioned incidents of discrimination, the White lesbians reacted most severely to sexual discrimination. In many cases, the internalization of sexual discrimination from
a combination of community and social sources exhausted them so
much that they did not have the energy to become mothers. In other
cases, lesbians translated their negative experiences into a belief that
it is unfair to raise children in a cruel, homophobic world.

Andrea, a middle-class White lesbian, talked about her partner who
had children from a previous heterosexual marriage. She had seen
how her partner's children were teased at school because of their
mother's sexual identity. Andrea, who wavered in her decision to remain childfree, saw sexual discrimination as an overwhelming force
that ultimately quelled any desire she had to become a mother:

> I think that I could've been on the fence. Had there been more
> societal, family, job support, had the situation been conducive,
> that that would have possibly been enough to sway me. But I
> just saw that it would have been battle after battle after battle.
> And I didn't think that I was up for that. Nor did I feel like I
> wanted to impose that on the child, either. I would be a de-
> cent mother, but I didn't think I would be an excellent enough
> mother to be able to counteract the crap that my child would get
> from the greater community. And I think basically I decided
> that my maternal instincts and my desire to have children were
> not strong enough to counteract those negatives. To me, in our
> community, it's not something that is an easy decision. It's not

like, "Oops, I'm pregnant." You know, it's something that takes a tremendous amount of thought and work, and if you're neutral you're never going to have a child. I don't really see myself as really anti-children, I see myself as kind of neutral. I don't have the oomph to go do all the work that it would take to either get a sperm donor or to find someone to be a father and then deal with all of that. I mean, when I start thinking about how wonderful it would be to have a child, I start thinking about all this other crap, and all of a sudden I'm back to that neutral position again.

Andrea's comments reveal how ambivalent she was in her decision and how sexual discrimination, coupled with a lack of social support, dampened any desires she once had for becoming a mother.

Working-class White lesbians also described how sexual discrimination affected their decisions. Many working-class White lesbians raised concerns similar to Andrea's, indicating how difficult it was to be a lesbian:

MABEL: I guess my decision to not have children is to not put a child into that position if I can prevent it. And I can't prevent who I am to other people's children, but I can prevent what circumstances I would put my own into.

EVE: I would agree with that, definitely. I wouldn't put a child into a situation that would cause them more anguish.

MABEL: Right. Same way I would not choose to be gay if I had a choice. This would not be a life I would choose if I could choose.

These remarks about what it means to be gay and how participants feel about being gay are both powerful and sad. Although many lesbians indicated pride in their lesbian identities, Mabel's comments reveal how a hostile world forces some lesbians to struggle with their personal and sexual identities. In many ways, sexual discrimination created a structure of constraints that deterred some lesbians from becoming mothers and thus, by default, encouraged them to remain childfree.

In addition to being discouraged from motherhood by sexual discrimination, working-class White lesbians differed from their middle-class counterparts in that they held the view that the world in general was an ugly place. This "ugly worldview" originated in particular social experiences and understandings of social problems such as overpopulation and crime. Mabel summed up what others in her group also expressed:

> I think there's enough kids in the world already. And I love
> children. I'm involved with my nieces and nephews, too, but
> I just think there's enough. I think this world is a crazy world
> that we live in. And with the guns and the drugs and all the
> horrible things that happen, I don't think bringing a child into
> this world is necessarily a good thing. I don't know that I could
> protect a child enough to eliminate heart attack for myself.
> Maybe it's a selfish thing, but I just think there's enough kids
> in this world. And we have a horrible world that we live in right
> now. It's just my opinion.

In addition to drugs, crime, and overpopulation, a few working-class White lesbians also mentioned HIV/AIDS as contributing to their view that the world is too harsh for children. Kerry explained that the experience of temporarily mothering her nephews instilled in her a fear of HIV/AIDS that affected her decision to remain childfree:

> I would look at it as where Mabel was saying, where it's a bad
> world we're living in. Because [the boys] were pre-teens when
> they moved in and I went through the puberty thing with my
> oldest nephew. It's scary to think as a parent that—I mean,
> kids will be kids, you know. Kids will be kids and boys will be
> boys. They're going to go out and do whatever they want any-
> way, whether you tell them not to or not, and it is scary because
> you're going to lose that person eventually. And the thought of
> AIDS in that manner does affect my decision because I don't
> want to go through that. I mean, everybody dies sooner or later,
> but that is an extremely hard thing to go through, and I don't
> want to be there.

Later in the interview Kerry stated that the fear of losing a child was her principal reason for wanting to remain childfree. Because as an aunt she had no custody rights over her nephews when the court ordered them to return to their parents, in a very real way Kerry had already lost her children. She was not willing to go through that experience again, particularly given her view of the world as a scary and dangerous place. The combination of her "ugly worldview" and her past experiences shifted Kerry's desire to be a mother toward a decision to remain childfree.

It is not surprising that the working-class White lesbians in my study expressed concerns about violence, drugs, environmental problems, and HIV/AIDS. People from working-class White families are particularly sensitive to social and economic changes because such changes force them to consider their own social and economic vulnerability. Feeling that their racial privilege is compromised by the constraints of their class, working-class White Americans can come to focus on the negative aspects of the social world (L. Rubin, 1994). Translating this concern into motherhood, the working-class White lesbians in my study felt that bringing children into a world with so many problems would be unfair to the children, a feeling that encouraged some of them to remain childfree.

POSITIVE UNDERSTANDINGS OF
LESBIAN MOTHERHOOD

Despite many lesbians' dissatisfaction with, and concerns about, the lesbian baby boom, an important number of lesbians, including some who chose to remain childfree, spoke positively about lesbian motherhood. More than half the lesbians I interviewed provided positive responses, stating that lesbian mothers are emotionally strong, are changing the definition of motherhood in positive ways, have flexible roles within families, and teach their children to be open-minded to difference in general. They also acknowledged that society is more accepting of lesbian mothers as the definition of family changes. In addition, many lesbians in my study maintained that lesbian motherhood is good because lesbians make an intentional choice and are not forced into motherhood.

Even for some lesbians who originally did not want to become mothers, positive views of lesbian motherhood helped create a positive psychological space in which some ultimately decided to become mothers. This was particularly true when lesbians were able to renegotiate gender roles and develop positive understandings of motherhood through their own lesbian relationships. In my study, as lesbians began to experience intimate lesbian relationships, many began to realize that there are qualitatively significant differences between lesbian and heterosexual relationships. This was mostly true for middle-class lesbians, with variations by race. Many middle-class White lesbians found that the lesbian relationships they were in afforded a more equal and flexible division of labor, as well as more freedom to pursue personal goals, than did the heterosexual relationships they had previously experienced or witnessed. The equal and flexible nature of these lesbian relationships allowed middle-class White lesbians to revisit and renegotiate negative views of gender roles in families.

Because middle-class lesbians, regardless of race, were most likely to hold the view that motherhood is oppressive to women, middle-class lesbians were most likely to renegotiate views of motherhood once they became involved in lesbian relationships. June, a middle-class White lesbian, had "sworn up and down that I didn't want my mother's life," because she understood her mother's life to be oppressive. But as June explained, she was able to rethink her beliefs about motherhood because as an adult in a lesbian relationship, June understood that her mother and she did not live in the same family structure:

> When I was about 27 it hit me, and it took another thirteen
> years, but I think that [my mother's] idea and my idea of
> motherhood is somewhat similar. But her life and her way
> of being a mother was very much, you know, what I didn't
> want to do.

June changed her mind about becoming a mother when she realized that she could parent in a different way from her own mother; that is, June could mother as a lesbian within a lesbian relationship. To her that meant more freedom and choice than her own mother had within a heterosexual marriage. June and other middle-class White lesbians were able to renegotiate their views of their own mothers' experiences by redefining motherhood within a lesbian context.

As June's comment suggests, lesbians' experiences of their relationships as being more flexible than heterosexual ones allowed those who rejected heterosexual gender roles to consider becoming a mother. Kathy, a middle-class White lesbian mother, emphasized this point:

> When I had kids, it was within the lesbian framework. It wasn't like trying to make a wish come true and fit kind of an image I had and always wanted to get to within the male-female context. It was totally reframed because it was stripped. I mean, [age] 15–16 on I just thought, "No kids." And then, you know, at [age] 26–27, I'm like, "Whoa, maybe there's a reality to this with two women." And so having kids for me was within the context of with a female partner.

Kathy decided to have children after she realized she could be a mother as a lesbian and with a lesbian partner. Kathy also found that a lesbian relationship "changes that whole role thing" that exists in heterosexual couples. More specifically, lesbians are able to create a more equitable division of labor than heterosexual couples because there are no preconceived notions of what that division of labor should be.

Middle-class lesbians of color also discussed being able to see how lesbian relationships created space for them to become mothers. However, their reasons were different from those of their White counterparts. Whereas middle-class White lesbians grew up thinking heterosexual motherhood was oppressive, many middle-class lesbians of color grew up in families in which mothers had a lot of power and responsibility. As Beth, a middle-class Black lesbian (and Kathy's partner), explained, lesbian motherhood allowed her to have authority similar to her own mother's, something many middle-class lesbians of color wanted:

> We both cook. Kathy mows the lawn. I'm supposed to weed— see, "supposed to." You know, we have very distinct things: I like to cook, she likes to do this or the other, I like grocery shopping, she can't stand it, I mean, so you end up dividing

labor. But I don't look at it in the terms of the mom thing 'cause again, I was raised by a single mom. So I don't know if a dad would have gone out and went grocery shopping or he's the one who would have grilled.

Beth's comment suggests that being raised by a single-mother helped her develop a flexible sense of family division of labor, and lesbian motherhood allowed her to emulate that. Miriam, a middle-class Black lesbian and her partner, Desiree, a middle-class Latina, echoed Beth's comments. During the focus group, they discussed whether or not lesbian and heterosexual relationships are really that different:

DESIREE: There are differences, but they're not based on gender. I see our best friends, the men do all the cooking,
   they do laundry, they're the neat ones. Our girlfriends are
   spoiled. I'm like, "Man, I would've gone with a man if they
   were that good when I was out there looking for them." I
   mean, they have good men. They have really good men.

MIRIAM: But I think mothers have always been different things.
   But there's a stereotype that kind of pretends like mothers
   are one way, but because we're both women it kind of points
   out the fact that, you know, mothers can be different ways.
   I mean, like you say, the mothers that we know don't cook
   and clean, but that's not paid attention to because they're
   married to a man. And people see them as a man and a wife,
   and they assume that things are the way they think they
   are, but they're not really that way. You don't go into people's
   marriages and into their house and see what the mothers
   do and the fathers do. But I think that [lesbians just make it]
   more obvious.

DESIREE: And because we're women, our decisions, we've really gone back and forth. One worked full time, one stayed
   home, one's evening. I mean, we fluctuate a lot . . . I think
   we have more flexibility. There's not an expectation that I
   will always be the breadwinner. I don't feel that. In a couple
   years I could say, "You know what? Boom." And I think we

have that a little bit more [flexibility], whereas the men in our friendship group, I don't think they'd ever feel like they couldn't work. Whereas the women more, you know, there's certain things that I think are still there. Whereas for us, they aren't as rigid because there are two women. Yeah, I think so.

Desiree and Miriam make two important points. First, as Miriam stated, what people *think* happens in families and what really *does* happen may be different. Second, in heterosexual families, men may be more reluctant to give up their paid work. Even though some heterosexual families may not follow strict gendered divisions of labor, some gendered rules still apply. Although some lesbians rejected heterosexual gender roles early in their lives, they were able to renegotiate those roles to fit a more suitable role within a lesbian context. Renegotiating the gendered nature of families—or in essence, de-gendering families—and having positive experiences with, and ideas about, lesbian motherhood gave middle-class lesbians, regardless of race, incentive to become mothers.

CREATING AN UNDERSTANDING OF MOTHERHOOD

Beliefs about motherhood that exist in particular communities and in the larger society, coupled with lesbians' gendered and sexual experiences, created an understanding of motherhood that lesbians weighed in their decisions to become mothers or remain childfree. For many lesbians in my study, beliefs about motherhood played an important role in their decision-making processes. All of the lesbians in my study who rejected pregnancy, adoption, or the basic notion of lesbian motherhood decided to remain childfree. Although some who held positive views of lesbian motherhood chose to remain childfree, only lesbians who developed positive ideas about lesbian motherhood were able to make the psychological leap into motherhood.

Because beliefs about motherhood varied among particular communities, the beliefs that lesbians interviewed for this study held about pregnancy, adoption, and lesbian motherhood varied by race and class. White lesbians, regardless of class, were most likely to state that they did not want to become pregnant. Averse to pregnancy after having seen other women give birth, or hoping for partners who might want to give birth, these lesbians rejected pregnancy for themselves. Working-class lesbians, regardless of race, were most likely to reject adoption because they feared the biases of the legal system, including adoption agencies, lawyers, and courts. They also recognized the financial burdens of adoption and pregnancy and equated lesbian motherhood with middle-class privilege. Regardless of race and class, several lesbians in my study believed that lesbian motherhood is an avenue that lesbians take to gain heterosexual privilege. However, in recognizing that lesbian motherhood is a class privilege, working-class lesbians raised the point that heterosexual privilege is most likely to be gained through class privilege.

Sexual discrimination was a factor that often led to a negative view of lesbian motherhood, a view that also varied by race and class. White lesbians, regardless of class, reacted most overtly to sexual discrimination and seemed to internalize the sexual discrimination they experienced. Perhaps because of race privilege, White lesbians seemed more surprised by, and less prepared for, sexual discrimination than lesbians of color. The result was a more prominent discussion among White lesbians of how sexual discrimination, along with other negative social factors, created a world in which they might not want to raise children, and therefore why they chose to remain childfree. However, Roxanne's comments reveal that race, gender, and sexual discrimination intersect to shape the experiences of lesbians of color as well. Roxanne had clearly spent time thinking about the many axes of discrimination in her life that ultimately led her to decide to remain childfree.

Despite the negative views of motherhood held by nearly half the lesbians in my study, most of the lesbians I interviewed understood lesbian motherhood within a positive framework. This sentiment was shared mostly by lesbians who ultimately decided to become mothers, but also by some who remained childfree. Like those who held negative views, those who held positive views also varied by race and class. Middle-class White lesbians focused on how lesbian motherhood offered a non-gendered division of labor that moved away from their vision of motherhood as oppressive and restrictive. Middle-class lesbians of color also focused on the flexibility of lesbian families and motherhood. But they did so because they were pleased to find that their own families could emulate the flexibility of their mothers' families within a lesbian context.

Regardless of whether lesbians developed negative or positive understandings of lesbian motherhood, these understandings shaped their mothering decisions in important ways. Often in subtle ways, lesbians carefully examined how gender, sexuality, race, and class connected to create others', as well as their own, beliefs about lesbian motherhood. Combined with the support and constraints from other social factors such as social networks, intimate relationships, and work (factors I discuss in the following three chapters), understandings of lesbian motherhood work in concert to shape the decision-making processes that lesbians go through to decide whether to become mothers or remain childfree.

CHAPTER SIX

Negotiating Lesbian Support Networks

In order to actualize their mothering desires, lesbians seek support from a variety of social networks, one of the most important of which comes from lesbian communities. Lesbians who want to remain childfree look to other childfree lesbians for social outlets and emotional support. Lesbians who want to become mothers look to lesbian mothers who can lend them emotional support and help them through the process of becoming a mother. Lesbian networks help cushion the blow of homophobic families and communities of origin, heterosexist policies, and external homophobic attitudes that can wear lesbians down, regardless of their mothering decisions. For lesbians of color, support networks also create a cushion against a world that discriminates along multiple axes of race, class, gender, and sexuality. This chapter examines women's relationships to lesbian social networks and how lesbians weigh those relationships in their decisions to become mothers or remain childfree.

Throughout their history, lesbians have created social networks that revolve around community building, educating the public, taking political and legal action, and providing social support for lesbians themselves (Dunne, 2000; Morningstar, 1999). For many lesbians, however, any one network rarely provides all the support they need.

Because of this, they often rely upon a variety of networks. However, this can cause friction as support networks may collide with, and contradict, one another. For example, lesbians of color may find networks that support them along lines of sexuality, but not race, and vice versa.

Social networks for lesbians of color can clash with one another because of racial discrimination within larger LGBT communities and homophobia within communities of origin (Bennett and Battle, 2001; Lee, 1992; Mays, Cochran, and Rhue, 1993; Morales, 1990; Rust, 2006; B. Smith, 1998). The result is that lesbians of color sometimes exist in the borderlands between communities of color and lesbian communities (Anzaldúa, 1999). Living within these borderlands, lesbians often create their own social support networks (Silvera, 1995) or they choose one support network over another. Not only divided along racial lines, lesbian communities are divided along class lines as well (Kennedy and Davis, 1993). Unlike those in the borderlands, lesbians who are privileged along lines of race and class are more likely to be centrally located and better integrated into social networks that support most of their needs.

In addition to being divided by race and class, lesbian communities are also divided by mothering decisions. As discussed in chapter 1, there is an ideological division within larger lesbian communities regarding lesbian motherhood, with some believing that lesbians are transforming motherhood by overcoming a patriarchal family structure, and others believing that lesbian mothers are assimilating into a heterosexual and patriarchal institution in an effort to gain heterosexual privilege. Concurrent with the debate about transformation and assimilation, lesbian communities are also divided on the basis of logistics. Much like heterosexual mothers, lesbian mothers are much more tied to their children's schedules and needs, and therefore tend to be less spontaneous and flexible, than childfree lesbians. Much like childfree heterosexual women, childfree lesbians do not need to build into their own time someone else's nap schedule, play dates, school hours, or illnesses. They are much more flexible as to when they can go out, where they can go, and how long they can stay.

In order to accommodate the growing number of lesbian mothers and to create a space for their families within lesbian communities, lesbians have developed social networks specifically to meet their parenting needs. This development was enhanced by responses to the HIV/AIDS epidemic, which provided general meeting places for lesbians and other LGBT community members. Many organizations that originally focused on the epidemic "began offering other social services, such as parenting and support groups" (Pollack, 1995, p. 99). As a result, since the early 1980s regional and national lesbian and gay parenting groups have burgeoned all over the United States, creating a structure of emotional, legal, and informational support for LGBT parents. In addition, local, regional, and national networking has allowed lesbian mothers to come out in large numbers to educate the public, promote positive images of lesbian families, and dispel myths about their families perpetuated by right-wing religious leaders and conservative social scientists (Pollack, 1995).

Because of the divisions within larger lesbian communities, and because the lives of most lesbians are multifaceted, in my study most lesbians were integrated into a variety of social networks involving a combination of friends, family, and community. The social support that they received in their mothering decisions was not only closely related to how easy or difficult it was for them to come out to families and communities of origin but also to the types of lesbian networks they had access to by virtue of race, class, and mothering decision.

NEGOTIATING DIVIDED LESBIAN COMMUNITIES

The lesbians in my study discussed clear divisions within larger lesbian communities, not only along lines of race and class but also along lines of motherhood. Middle-class lesbians, regardless of race, were integrated into and supported by formal lesbian networks. These networks greatly facilitated their mothering decisions, both to become mothers and to remain childfree. For middle-class lesbians who wanted to become mothers, lesbian support networks offered crucial information about how to become a mother as well as emotional support that these women did not always receive elsewhere. Kathy, a middle-class White lesbian who was among the first lesbians in her community to have children, discussed how even the few lesbian mothers she knew early on helped shape her decision:

I'm in a moms group. I'm in two moms groups, and one is a lesbian parenting one and one is a mixed one. And in the mixed one, there's eleven families. Four of them are lesbian families, but the others are not. If I was not in this college-based community that had a large lesbian community that I'd been a part of, that I knew people were—at that time it was just insemination, although since then there's been a lot of adoptions. If I didn't have that right here locally, I might not have [become a mother]. If I had been in [a more isolated town] at the time, it might not have even crossed our paths till way past the clock was ticking. So I think it had an impact— where I lived and kind of the trends of the lesbian community in this country, um, definitely had an impact. Right place / right time kind of thing.

Other middle-class lesbians expressed similar sentiments: that because there were many lesbians in the area having children, and because those lesbians were well organized, lesbian networks provided a structure of opportunities (Gerson, 1985) through which they themselves could become mothers. In areas well populated with other lesbian mothers, the effort to have children did not feel like a continuous battle. Even if families or communities did not support lesbians, being supported by the lesbian mother community was often enough to give lesbians the help they needed to fulfill their desires to become mothers. For example, Anita, a middle-class Latina lesbian who experienced great resistance from her family and community of origin, acknowledged the importance of her connections to the lesbian community in her town:

For me, because my family wasn't that supportive, it was my friends, and it was very important to me to hang out with, um, I got into the lesbian moms group before I adopted Jonathon, and it was part torture, part—you know, great to be around lesbian moms and all the kids, but it was a long one-and-a-half years before I got Jonathon. And it continued to be wonderful to have that group of people after I got Jonathon.

Anita explained that her children have complicated medical problems. While some of her heterosexual friends thought she was "nuts" for adopting so many special-needs children, her friends within the lesbian community continued to support her. As she recalled, she had "a good group of friends that stayed close, and finally kind of normalized my life, my family." Anita's comments summarize the benefits of being connected to strong lesbian mother networks. Such networks fill in when family, community, and childfree and heterosexual friends are not supportive. They normalize each other's lives and families in ways that allow lesbians to feel secure and integrated into a healthy community for them and their children. For most of the lesbians in my study, personal desire alone did not provide enough support for them to become mothers.

Although lesbians found support among other lesbians, there were divisions within communities based on mothering decisions. As Rita, a middle-class White lesbian, described, she did not realize that this divide existed until after she decided to adopt a child:

> It was very difficult because the part of the community I was in, I didn't realize, they're not anti-kids, but there is no room in their life for kids. So it's been total, total social change for me. I was a lot in the sports community, and people who I thought would really be around and be excited 'cause they don't have to parent, they just have to be around, you know, I thought they'd be excited. But they don't even have room for that. And so it was really a big change for me, a huge change. And I would do it again anyway, but I didn't foresee it. I didn't see that having a kid would make my life that much different, that it would change friendships so much. But it has. Luckily I've found enough other parents that it's worked out well, but it was a huge change.

Despite the lack of support Rita received from childfree lesbians, she was able to find lesbian mothers in her area who supported her decision and her new family. My findings suggest that this advantage comes directly from class privilege. As discussed later in this chapter, working-class lesbians were not nearly as "lucky."

Middle-class lesbians, regardless of race, who wanted to remain childfree also discussed the importance of lesbian networks. They spoke of the support that other childfree lesbians provided them, as well as how lesbian mothers and childfree lesbians negotiated their different positions within the larger lesbian community. Middle-class lesbians pointed out that both groups lead somewhat separate but occasionally overlapping lives. They said that although most of their friends were childfree, at times they socialized with lesbian mothers and their children. Most childfree middle-class lesbians respected the decisions of their friends who became mothers and were still willing to socialize with them. Amy, a middle-class Black lesbian, discussed the debate surrounding motherhood, and her appreciation for that debate, within the larger middle-class lesbian community:

> This is so wonderful 'cause I think about my friends who said they would never [become a mother] and used to call women who had children "breeders." Those same women are having [children], and with such a slap in the face. If you were a pioneering lesbian who wanted a child, you were looked down upon in the community as selling out, as becoming part of this, this— you were being heterosexual-like. Well, you know, that's how we determine your sexuality, not how we determine how you parent. And so I think what's happened is sort of funny, because now they're having this major debate in the community itself about, well, are you really a lesbian if you choose to have children and to live in a home and to parent those children like straight people? So I love it. I love the debate. I'm excited about it.

Because middle-class lesbians had more resources than working-class lesbians, including support networks, they were able to appreciate the debate and not have it tear their communities apart. Barb, a middle-class White lesbian who had wanted to become a mother but decided to remain childfree, stated:

> I run in the same crowd that Judy and Tammy run in. And I think we make a special effort sometimes in saying that children can come and other times when we don't want children. We made the decision that it's not appropriate to have children at other times, like on poker night. Yeah, poker night. It's not a good night to have kids. And the group camping trips are

sometimes not a good time for kids. But then there are other times when they're openly welcome.

Judy seemed less willing than Barb to have children around, although she stated that her expanded circle of friends has children and "we like them anyway." Tammy said that sometimes she likes having children around because "it's a change to see a different lifestyle."

As this discussion suggests, middle-class childfree lesbians, regardless of race, exercised control over their social groups. And as Amy stated, the debate within the community was enjoyable, providing some intellectual stimulus. Control over social networks and the ability to turn a potentially divisive debate into an intellectual one allowed middle-class lesbians to find support for their decisions to remain childfree. Support from other childfree lesbians also reinforced decisions to remain childfree. Many lesbians in my study said they wanted to remain childfree because they desired personal freedom. The ability to control their social lives satisfied part of this desire.

In contrast to middle-class lesbians, working-class lesbians had a more mixed relationship to lesbian networks that varied largely by race and mothering decision. Working-class lesbians of color who wanted to remain childfree were integrated into supportive LGBT and heterosexual communities. Unlike their middle-class counterparts, this group of lesbians relied heavily on a variety of social networks, rather than just on lesbian ones, for support of their childfree lives. As Sara, a working-class Latina, explained:

> I'm very active, but I mesh with the gay community. I mean, I have a well- balanced life. I'm very active with my family. I have straight friends; I have gay friends. I mostly hang out with my gay friends, but I do have straight friends, and I'm very active. I go to a lot of the gay functions, you know. We are very social. I'm a very social person. Every Friday and Saturday night, Thursday night, we're gone doing things, and I feel that I'm very out there. Definitely!

When I asked Sara if she thought that being integrated into different communities affected her decision to remain childfree, she stated that what she liked about being childfree was the freedom to be able to join whatever communities she wanted. Her response shows a relationship between being childfree and having varied social networks. On the one hand, the freedom of not having children allowed her to be social. On the other hand, the availability of social networks supporting her decision to be childfree gave her the sense of freedom she desired. Terry, a working-class Black lesbian, also described her integration into multiple social networks. This strategy was one working-class lesbians of color used to increase their support in a world of limited options.

Unlike working-class lesbians of color who wanted to remain childfree, working-class lesbians of color who wanted to become mothers found it harder to access lesbian networks, which made it more difficult for them to realize their desires to become mothers. Neither Joy, Kizzy, nor Diane, all working-class Black lesbians, were integrated into or supported by any formal lesbian mother network or group. Like the childfree working-class lesbians of color, Joy was integrated into a network of *childfree* lesbians and gay men. But she knew of only a few lesbian mothers and was not closely connected with any of them. Kizzy and Diane had lesbian friends who were trying to have children, so they were able to tap into them as a source of support. However, they were not part of a formal support group or network. As Kizzy explained, the lack of support made it difficult for them to locate the necessary information and services, such as "lesbian-friendly" doctors (i.e., physicians willing to inseminate lesbians or order sperm for them so they could inseminate at home), needed for them to become mothers:

> It seems to me very much piecemeal. You have to find out whatever you can find out wherever you can. 'Cause I was looking on the Internet and had this one search engine that claims to have a listing of gay-friendly doctors, and so I looked for [our area], and it didn't. I was just like, "Oh." I think a more formal network, even if it was just a support group or somebody who was willing to be a resource, would be good.

Given my own familiarity with and integration into formal lesbian mother networks in the geographical area in which Kizzy lived, I was surprised by her statement that pertinent information was "piecemeal" and lacked a formal structure. Kizzy and Diane were equally surprised when I told them that formal networks existed in their town. As working-class lesbians of color, middle-class networks were invisible and inaccessible to them. Because Kizzy and Diane were not integrated into any formal lesbian mother networks, the Internet became an important resource for them. However, Kizzy and Diane's experience raises questions as to whether or not online resources provide the same kind of support as in-person support. In addition to the lack of integration into lesbian networks, the lack of knowledge about how to access important resources can deter lesbians from becoming mothers. Kizzy wanted to become a mother but had decided not do so. Then she realized that maybe she could:

> Most of my decision not to become a parent was because I felt like I didn't have a real support system, so that has always been sort of a prerequisite in my mind to belong to a larger community and to have a larger support system. So I felt like I have a little bit more of that now, so I think that's helpful.

As Kizzy's comment illustrates, social support networks within lesbian communities give many lesbians what they need to turn their mothering *desire* into a mothering *decision*. The lack of such support for working-class lesbians of color contributes to them delaying their decisions to become mothers or even deciding to remain childfree. It also suggests one possible reason why I had such difficulty recruiting lesbian mothers from working-class communities of color into my study. Because of a lack of support, there may be a limited number of working-class lesbians of color who actually become mothers.

Much like working-class lesbians of color, working-class White lesbians also had a mixed relationship with lesbian support networks. However, for them the gulf between lesbian mothers and childfree lesbians ran particularly deep and was not easily bridged. Whereas childfree working-class lesbians of color found support in a variety of networks, working-class White lesbians looked primarily to lesbian networks and found little support there for their desires to remain childfree. Nearly every childfree working-class White lesbian in my study complained about how the rift in the community limited their choice of lesbian friends, leaving them with little control over their social lives. Kerry, who had gained and then lost custody of her nephews prior to the interview, found that the community of lesbians she was integrated into was not accepting of diverse mothering decisions:

> Growing up in the beginning of our relationship [my partner and I] never really dealt with other lesbians at all. In fact, she was the only other lesbian I knew. But after I started working where I do, I got into contact with some others, and we've become friends. And just as we were getting to know more lesbians and actually interacting in the community . . . , that's when the kids entered our picture. And when the kids entered our picture it was like, boom, that [lesbian community] was gone again. And then now that the kids have moved back out, it's hard. It's hard for us to touch back into that [community] because it was like we were automatically shut out. You know you lose your contact with your friends being childless and having children. They are completely different, and that's like our lives. When it happened, we're like turned upside down and sideways and about 360 degrees the other way. And that is exactly what happened to us and now we're actually having a hard time getting back into that circuit because . . . it comes back to harsh words. But if they threw you out of the community because you were having kids, why would you want to go back? Why go back?

Perhaps one reason why working-class White childfree lesbians did not want to spend time with lesbian mothers is that they felt pressure to have children from those lesbians. In Kerry's case, she lost support when she became a mother and felt pressure to remain childfree. However, some working-class White childfree lesbians, such as Mabel, felt pressure from lesbian mothers to become mothers:

> I'm feeling [social pressure]. We had [lesbian] friends of ours that had twins, and we felt it, me and my partner, when they had their commitment ceremony. "Why aren't you guys hav-

ing a commitment ceremony?" "Well, we decided not to." And
now they're having children. "Well, why aren't you guys having kids? You've been together more than five to six years. You
should be having a family now." And so we feel that pressure
especially in today's environment. And now we're even feeling
it even more with the children and commitment ceremonies,
and society's norms even for lesbians now are becoming pressure to answer that question.

As new family choices became available to lesbians, and as lesbian
motherhood became more accepted not only by lesbians themselves
but also by larger society, the working-class White lesbians I interviewed felt a new pronatalist pressure. Clara explained that such pressure from within lesbian communities was recent. She stated that
"ten years ago it was all about just having fun. You know, finding out
who you were." Pronatalism within the community meant, therefore,
that working-class White lesbians were forced to frequently revisit and
defend their decisions to remain childfree.

For middle-class White lesbians, control over their social networks
was something they took for granted. Middle-class White lesbians were
not resentful toward lesbian mothers because they had a large middle-
class childfree lesbian community from which they could gain support. The smaller, more divided working-class White childfree lesbian
community felt restricted and confined by the intrusion of, and social
pressure created by, lesbian mothers. Discussions among working-
class White childfree lesbians suggest that the divide in the community based on mothering decisions leaves working-class White lesbians with limited support, particularly for those who want to remain
childfree.

Pronatalism within working-class White lesbian communities
worked to the advantage, however, of lesbians who wanted to become
mothers. Whereas most working-class lesbians of color were not well
integrated into a lesbian mother network, most working-class White
lesbians were. For example, Sadie and Janet were active participants
in formal lesbian mother groups. Janet had been integrated into the
larger lesbian community for many years and entered the lesbian

mother community after her partner had their first son. Because they recognized a growing interest in motherhood, Janet and her partner helped organize a formal lesbian mother support group:

> There was a group of us that were trying to get pregnant or had just had children, and we decided we wanted to get together every month for support, and we had been doing that up to the last year. But when we first started there were maybe eight women, four families and one single parent meeting, and I think there were two children at the time. And now there are fourteen women, close to thirty-some children.

Janet's comment not only shows how rapidly the lesbian mother community in her area was growing but also how lesbian mothers create networks to support themselves.

Regarding lesbian networks, Martha was the one exception among working-class White lesbians in my study. During the interview, she shared that she was not integrated into a lesbian mother group. As with Kizzy and Diane, the lack of integration made it hard for her to find a doctor to help her with donor insemination. When I asked Martha what events led up to her decision to be a mother, she responded:

> I've just, ever since I was young I've, I've wanted to have kids, and actually it was after meeting you that, when you told me about the artificial insemination through [the doctor you used], that gave me, "Okay, I definitely have an option of someone that's okay with doing this to go and try it." So it was actually knowing of a doctor willing to do it. I called around and talked to probably about ten or fifteen [physicians], and they just weren't willing to do it unless it was a father going to be the donor.

My being well connected helped Martha because I was able to pass on to her information I had gathered from the lesbian network. However, her lack of integration meant that she spent a lot of time and energy trying to locate resources that middle-class lesbians and some working-class White lesbians easily found through formal lesbian mother groups. Her lack of integration, and therefore lack of access to important knowledge, delayed her attempt to become a mother.

USING NETWORKS TO ACCESS PHYSICIANS AND CONCEPTIVE TECHNOLOGIES

As Martha's comments illustrate, lesbians' access to, and experience with, medical professionals was closely related to how well integrated they were into lesbian networks. Much like participants in previous studies (Lasker, 1998), several of the participants in my study reported difficulties in finding general physicians and fertility specialists willing to work with lesbians. This was important because the majority of the lesbians in my study (12 out of 17) became mothers through donor insemination. Two, Miriam and Desiree, used a known donor and inseminated at home, but the remaining ten used or were planning to use physician-assisted donor insemination. Only five of the seventeen had adopted children.

Because most of the lesbians in my study became, or were planning to become, mothers through physician-assisted donor insemination, most of their discussion revolved around how to find lesbian-friendly physicians. Lesbian mother support groups provided vital information about which medical and legal resources to use and how to access them. Finding physicians, as well as adoption agencies, was fairly easy for well-networked lesbians. As Patricia, a middle-class White lesbian, explained, she and her partner found a physician through a lesbian mother group in which she was involved. The physician was located near her home and was lesbian-friendly:

I think in somewhat of a positive way I knew that there was at least one OB/GYN physician in town here who was a fertility specialist who was supportive. We had already made the decision, but it helped the decision along 'cause I knew that there was service available here locally that would be supportive, and that we wouldn't have to hassle with him. And, in fact, when I went in for my visit with him he brought in some med student or somebody was along, and I didn't quite know how to say, you know, what my status was, and he said something about, he said "partner," first of all, he didn't say "your husband." He said "your partner" or whatever, "your relationship status," and I kind of stumbled with it and he goes, "I take it your partner's a woman, then?" And it was sort of like, "Oh, thanks."

Patricia's comment shows how having real access to a lesbian-friendly physician was critical in actualizing her mothering decision. Patricia's story was not unusual for other middle-class White lesbians in my study.

Just as race and class privilege through lesbian mother support networks increased White lesbians' access to lesbian-friendly physicians, race and class subordination decreased access to such physicians for working-class lesbians of color. Joy, a working-class Black lesbian, explained that there were so many barriers to becoming a mother, not the least of which was how to get pregnant:

> There are a lot [of challenges to becoming a mother]. Who's going to be the father? Is it going to be someone that you know? How are you going to conceive? The sperm donation? . . . There's a lot of challenges. Am I going to wait until I'm in a stable relationship . . . or am I just going to do this on my own? I think that's the biggest challenge. And then after that falls, exactly how are you going to do it? Are you going to do the sperm donation thing? And then after you do that either way, what are you going to tell your parents? [laughs].

Later, in explaining how she tried to get pregnant, Joy added:

> Well, I had, I met a gentleman. He didn't really know that I was a lesbian. He knew I wanted children, and it was kind of trickery to it because he didn't know that I was trying to conceive. But that was my intention, my full intention, but it just never worked out.

After not getting pregnant and feeling bad that she had tried to trick a man into getting her pregnant, she decided to use donor insemination. Yet, as Joy explains, it was not easy to find a physician, particularly because her health insurance limited the physicians she could visit:

> JOY: Well right now I just started, I had been dealing with an HMO that kept you in a network for a long time, and I had

been experiencing, um, female-related problems, and by me not being able to get out of the circle of doctors in the HMO I could never get the problem taken care of. So when I switched jobs and was able to get with [my current insurance], and be able to go to any doctor that you want to, I began to see new doctors. So I have a doctor now, and actually he's corrected my female-related problem, which is a plus. Actually I do believe that he may know that I'm lesbian. I'm not sure, but he does all of the insemination, which was really, that was the first doctor I had ever ran into that did that. And I think that would probably be who I would go to.

NM: So do you think that that's influenced your decision at all, working with the medical community?

JOY: Yeah, actually. It has become a light at the end of the tunnel a little bit. Yeah.

NM: That you found someone who could actually make this happen if you want it, when you're ready to get pregnant.

JOY: And I probably can get it paid for through insurance, if I get it billed properly.

It was not until Joy switched to a job with more comprehensive health insurance coverage that she was able to find a physician who would address a reproductive health problem she was having and also inseminate her. Joy found a willing physician not through a lesbian mother network but through several years of searching and being constrained by her health insurance. Comparing Joy's experience with that of most White lesbians in my study, my findings suggest that Joy's initial overwhelming questions about how to get pregnant could have been answered more quickly and less painfully had she been integrated into a lesbian mother network.

Finding a lesbian-friendly physician was particularly important because most sperm banks will only send sperm to a physicians' office, not directly to the client. Therefore, finding a physician was often the only way lesbians could get pregnant without having to engage in sexual intercourse with a man. Although Joy was initially willing to get pregnant through heterosexual intercourse, most lesbians in my study did not see that as an option. Finding a physician gave lesbians access to new opportunities. Beth, a middle-class Black lesbian who was well integrated into a lesbian mother network, described how her childhood aspirations to be a mother had been squelched and then reignited when she and her partner realized that there were medical means available allowing lesbians to have children:

> Kids were the farthest thing at that point from [my] mind until we both started to recognize that this is a possibility, that you don't have to give up those childhood dreams because you're a lesbian. You don't have to give those things up.

Beth's statement shows that when lesbians succeed in gaining access to physicians and the conceptive technologies that physicians often control, they have a better chance of realizing their desire to mother. Not being well integrated into lesbian mother networks greatly reduced lesbians' chances of finding such physicians.

FITTING INTO COMMUNITIES AND ACCESSING SUPPORT

How lesbians are integrated into and gain access to lesbian networks is complicated and depends on race and class positions as well as mothering desires. I found that lesbians weigh two particularly important issues concerning lesbian networks in making their mothering decisions: how they fit into divided lesbian communities, and how they could access the support they needed to become mothers or remain childfree. Working-class White lesbians found lesbian communities to be divided along lines of mothering decisions. Those who were childfree felt resentment toward lesbian mothers. The result was to ostracize lesbians who decided to become mothers. In many ways, working-class White lesbians who wanted to become mothers found a more supportive niche within White lesbian mother communities— that is, if they were able to find and access them.

Working-class lesbians of color who wanted to remain childfree were very adept at accessing a variety of support networks, including lesbian and gay networks, that allowed them to live fulfilling lives without children. However, working-class lesbians of color who wanted to become mothers had difficulty finding and accessing lesbian mother communities. Their lack of integration, and therefore their lack of knowledge of necessary resources such as where to find lesbian-friendly physicians, deterred and delayed decisions to become mothers for some working-class lesbians of color.

Middle-class lesbians of color, regardless of mothering decision, were able to access lesbian support networks that had fluid boundaries between childfree lesbians and lesbian mothers. The lack of rigid boundaries meant that middle-class lesbians of color were able to socialize among a variety of lesbians, thus creating a wider system of support outside their families and communities of origin. Similarly, middle-class White lesbians were able to easily access lesbian networks, both for childfree lesbians and lesbian mothers. These two networks were somewhat mixed. However, middle-class White lesbians had control over when they wanted to integrate the two groups and when they wanted to keep them separate. There was no community hostility expressed by any of the middle-class lesbians, regardless of race.

As this chapter demonstrates, lesbians' access to, integration into, and experiences with lesbian support networks varied greatly by race, class, and mothering decision. My findings suggest, therefore, that lesbians constrained by race and class often feel isolated and even shunned by certain factions within lesbian communities. This is not to say that such communities do not offer support to those within them. However, the support can be limited because of how those communities have historically been shaped and divided by race, class, and mothering decision, as well as how they are currently being reshaped by the new family choices available to lesbians. Furthermore, how lesbians find, access, and fit into lesbian communities shapes their mothering decisions.

CHAPTER SEVEN

Weighing Intimate Partner Relationships

Having or not having an intimate partner was the factor the lesbians I interviewed most readily identified as influencing their decisions to become mothers or remain childfree. Intimate relationships greatly influence decisions to mother or remain childfree, regardless of sexuality, although the ways in which they do so vary by sexual identity as well as by race and class. For example, among heterosexuals, fragile or impermanent relationships often lead middle-class and working-class White women to remain childfree. Without a strong marriage, motherhood does not seem to be a true option for them (Gerson, 1985). Among poor Black women, however, this is not necessarily the case. Whereas White women see independence and strength along with a lack of a stable partner as reasons not to have children, Black women stress that their own independence and strength mean that they do not need permanent partners in order to successfully mother their children (Blum and Deussen, 1996).

For some heterosexual women, strong relationships with men can also prompt them to remain childfree. Women who have strong relationships with their husbands often do not want to disrupt those relationships. In addition to the fear of changing the division of labor at home and compromising family finances, many women fear that the presence of children will detract from the close interpersonal and sexual relationships they have with their husbands (Faux, 1984; Gerson, 1985). Men's parenting desires may also influence heterosexual women's decisions to become mothers. In particular, fear of losing a spouse or partner with strong parenting desires encourages women who may not personally desire children to become mothers in order to satisfy the desires of their husbands (Gerson, 1985).

As with heterosexual women, the attitude of partners can influence lesbians' mothering decisions. Many lesbian couples break up after disagreeing about whether or not to have children (Martin, 1993; Morningstar, 1999; Pies, 1988; Silber, 1991). Couples must negotiate who will birth or adopt the child. Once decided, negotiating the relationship of both partners to the child is of particular concern (Dunne, 2000). In addition, very few states allow second-parent adoptions where same-sex couples can adopt children together, creating a legal two-parent family Moskovitz, 1995; Stacey, 1996). Therefore, lesbian couples in which one partner has adopted or birthed the child need to discuss the role and relationship of the "other" mother (Muzio, 1999; Sullivan, 2004). For some couples this is not a difficult issue to resolve. For others, it can create great divides between partners (Martin, 1993; Pies, 1988; Silber, 1991). Lesbians who become pregnant using a known donor or through a previous heterosexual relationship face additional concerns. Not only do they need to negotiate their and their partner's relationship (if a partner is present), but they must also negotiate the role of the donor or father (Lewin, 1993).

The lesbians I interviewed revealed three main ways in which they weighed intimate partner relationships in making their mothering decisions. Some lesbians who were ambivalent or really did not want to have children found that their partners encouraged them to become mothers. Some lesbians who wanted to be mothers or were ambivalent about motherhood found that their intimate partners encouraged them to remain childfree. And in other instances, lesbians found that their desire to become a mother or remain childfree was not influenced by their intimate partner relationships at all. This chapter looks at these three situations to understand how lesbians weigh the desires of their intimate partners in relation to their own desires, and how they ultimately draw on their relationships to make a decision to become a mother or remain childfree.

PARTNERS WHO ENCOURAGE LESBIANS TO REMAIN CHILDFREE

Many of the lesbians in my study described how their intimate partner relationships encouraged them to remain childfree. Although the decision to remain childfree was affected by how much the individual wanted to become a mother, the bottom line was that many lesbians did not want to be single parents. Some lesbians who really wanted to become mothers decided to remain childfree because they did not find the right partner at the right time. Although both working- and middle-class lesbians said this, the meaning of the "right" partner and the "right" time differed by class. For middle-class lesbians, the right partner was someone who was emotionally stable, who was willing to commit to the relationship, and who wanted to have children. The right time was a time in a lesbian's life when she was ready to settle down and was not too old to mother. Barb, a middle-class White lesbian, had a strong desire to mother but ultimately decided to remain childfree. She said that not finding the right partner at the right time was the most salient factor in preventing her from becoming a mother:

> I always thought I wanted to be a parent and be involved in that. Through my various relationships, most of them have not wanted to have children. The one that did want to have children, fortunately I had the foresight to see that was not a good relationship, or a healthy individual, so the relationship ended. And now [my current partner] was married and had two children from that and is definitely over any child-rearing things. So we may do things with the grandchildren and that's it. Had I been involved in a relationship I probably would have very easily, could have been, in a parent relationship right now.

For Barb, the right person (i.e., her current partner) came along at the wrong time (i.e., after her partner had already had children). But it is clear from Barb's comment that she always planned on having children. Because she did not find a willing or stable partner earlier in her life, she did not actualize her desire to mother.

Much like Barb, several working-class lesbians who were financially stable and had health insurance also decided to remain childfree because they did not have a partner. For example, Joy, a working-class Black lesbian, was originally ambivalent about motherhood but then decided to have children despite health problems. However, as she explained, trying to become a mother without a partner ultimately discouraged her original plans:

> I actually enjoy my story. After getting the donor listing, I began discussing my plan with my [physician]. He stated that my condition [endometriosis] produced complications with actually getting pregnant. He stated that my plan, though a good one, might still not help me produce. I went ahead and had the procedure [laparoscopy] and while off work and watching the news I saw the most adorable dog on television who I rushed off and adopted. After a month of being a new puppy owner I knew that he was child enough for me. He is now 3½ years old and has settled quite a bit, but I have since had a hysterectomy. I would still love to have a child, but I do not want to be a single parent . . . I was single [when I tried to get pregnant] and though I had begun the process, I think that I may have been more inclined to follow through had I been partnered.

For Joy, the combination of not having a partner when she was trying to get pregnant, having endometriosis (which often prevents women from getting pregnant), and finding a puppy that took up much of her "mothering" time and need, discouraged her from becoming a mother.

Other working-class lesbians, however, were not as fortunate as Joy in that they were less financially stable and did not have good health insurance. For them, the "right" partner needed to be both emotionally and financially stable. In addition, the financially "right" time needed to correspond with the "right" time of wanting to have children. Pam, a middle-class Latina who came from a working-class background, said that at age 42—much to her surprise—she felt a biological urge to get pregnant but had to fight those urges because of her social situation:

For the first time in my life it was like biologically it almost felt like my eggs were crying out, "It's now or never." You know, like actually having a biological urge to duplicate yourself. And I had never had that feeling before. I didn't have it when I was young. It's just like, let's get pregnant. You know, your body's saying let's get pregnant. And then I just decided, "No, you're not doing this now. You're just, you're not going to do it. It would be selfish." I decided it would be selfish of me to do it at that time when I was feeling this urge to do it and didn't have a partner. I think not having a partner was a really big influence on my decision in two ways. One is I have seen people raising children, and I see how much sleep they don't get. And I think trying to do it alone—I know people do it alone and they do great jobs, but boy, to have a partner, to have someone to help you raise that child. I think I would need to have someone else that you can share the joys and the responsibilities with. And the other thing, it's combined with matters of money. If you have another person, then you have more income. 'Cause you're probably—with lesbians, you're probably both going to be work-ing, or if one of them is staying home then that probably means the other person has a pretty good job and health benefits . . . The older I get the more I'm concerned about having adequate health insurance . . . So I think . . . at the time that I was think-ing about [becoming a mother] and not having a partner really impacted on my decision. I think if I had been in a situation where I was with a partner and in a stable relationship, and we really loved each other and were in a position to have a child, I think my decision probably would have been different.

The combination of Pam's financial situation, her health insurance, and her lack of an intimate partner created constraints that ultimately outweighed her biological urge, and any emotional desires accompa-nying that urge, to have children.

For many working-class lesbians, the financial stability of her part-ner determined if this was the right one at the right time. The impor-tance of financial stability was crucial to many working-class lesbians because they understood the reality of economic hardship. They were very careful not to increase their economic hardships by having children or bringing a child into an economically strained situation. As Pam herself notes, it is a challenge to support a household on the salaries of two working women, unless one of them has a high income. But raising a child as a single parent adds a financial burden that many working-class lesbians did not want to incur. The result was that working-class definitions of the "right" partner have more criteria than those of middle-class lesbians, making it more difficult for the working-class lesbians in my study to become mothers. As discussed in chapter 3, the difficulty I had finding working-class mothers to participate in my study may be the result of a limited number of working-class lesbians who are willing and able to afford children.

Unlike those lesbians who really wanted to have children but ultimately chose not to because they did not find the right partner at the right time, another group of lesbians who were more ambivalent about motherhood said that if their partners had wanted children, they would have helped raise the child. However, they would not have taken the initiative themselves to become a mother. All of the lesbians who fell into this category were middle-class except for Terry, a working-class Black lesbian. Terry stated that she would be willing to parent, but only if both she and her partner were financially stable:

TERRY: If I were to meet anyone else, you know, another woman and she has a child, I would love that child just as well. I mean, there's nothing different about that. I'd help raise and support the child.

NM: And would you consider yourself to be a mother in that decision?

TERRY: Yes, I would.

NM: Are you partnered now?

TERRY: No, no. I need time for myself right now . . . I'm in a financial position to bring a child into the world. Yeah, I could, but then you have a partner too. You understand?

So that might put a little crunch, you know, and that's why I said my job . . . right now I want to be to where I'm making, like, fifty thousand a year. I mean that's real stable, you know? Thirty thousand is stable, but that's not enough . . . If I have a partner and they're not financially stable, then that won't work. I'll have these anxieties you know. [laughs] I'll have hangups, and I have to support this person as well because [in] my past relationship I basically helped my other partner get out of debt.

Terry also stated that her partner would have to be the one to birth the child because she had no interest in being pregnant. In order to decide to become a mother, Terry would need to be financially stable, have a financially stable partner, and have that partner birth a child. Because this was a tall order, Terry ultimately decided to remain childfree.

Unlike Terry, the remaining lesbians who said they would become mothers only if their partners wanted children were middle-class. Their class privilege reduced their concerns about finances and allowed them to focus on needing to be in love with their partner in order to decide to become mothers. This sentiment was expressed by middle-class lesbians, regardless of race. Roxanne and Amy, both middle-class Blacks who strongly identified as childfree, best expressed this:

AMY: Partner, no partner, I still would not be the one to have a child. [If my] partner would want a child? Fine with me. 'Cause I think I could be a good parent . . . In my [current] relationship, we both have discussed this one issue, and we choose not to have children.

ROXANNE: I'm sure maybe my viewpoint might be different if I was involved with someone, and they wanted to have a child. I really wouldn't want that, but what could I say if this person was someone that I loved, and they really wanted to have a child?

Several of the middle-class White lesbians who either wanted to be childfree or were ambivalent about motherhood also shared Amy and Roxanne's sentiments. Kristy summed it up well:

I never would have had a child of my own. If I'd gotten into a relationship with somebody who already had children, I would be willing to co-parent. But the choice for me would never have been to raise a child.

The middle-class lesbians who said they were willing to become mothers only if they had a partner whom they loved and who would take the initiative to mother all clearly stated that they were just as happy, and in fact preferred, to remain childfree. However, if they really loved their partner, they would not leave that partner because of the partner wanting children. In addition, they would help raise those children if that's what it took to stay together.

While there were lesbians who wanted to become mothers but never found the right partner, and there were others who did not want to mother unless strongly encouraged to by their partners, a third group of lesbians said that their partners already had children from previous heterosexual or lesbian relationships and therefore encouraged them to remain childfree. As with Barb's case, discussed above, because most of these partners did not want any more children, these lesbians had to choose between remaining with the partner or becoming mothers—and the partner often won. In these instances, even though their partners were mothers, the lesbians I interviewed were themselves not co-mothers, often because the children were already grown or because there was a divorced father involved who did not want to share parental responsibilities with his ex-wife's lesbian lover. Because courts often discriminate against lesbians in determining custody cases, many previously married lesbians try not to push their ex-husbands in this regard for fear of losing custody battles (Andrews, 1995; Arnup, 1995; Hartman, 1999; Moskovitz, 1996; Robson, 1992). This was true in my study as well, as Andrea, an ambivalent middle-class White lesbian, explained:

By the time that I got together with my partner, she had already been there, done it, had 'em. So I said, "Well, there'll always be grandchildren." I missed having the opportunity of knowing [her kids] when they were young, so I've never really bonded as a stepparent, particularly because when she and the kids moved in with me, her relationship with her ex-husband was very strained. So I mean, she had already been there . . . And there's enough difference in our ages. She's thirteen years older [than me], [so] she was already past that point of having a discussion. So it was never a real push to do it. But had I been with somebody different, it's possible I would have children.

Andrea's statement suggests that for lesbians who find partners who already have children, it is often more difficult for them to become mothers themselves, unless they decide to find another partner or be a single parent. For lesbians who want to remain childfree, there is no need to find another partner. But lesbians who want to mother or who are ambivalent about motherhood need to seriously weigh their intimate partner relationships if the partner already has children and does not want any more.

PARTNERS WHO ENCOURAGE LESBIANS TO BECOME MOTHERS

Just as intimate partners can encourage lesbians to remain childfree, they can also influence lesbians' decisions to become mothers. This was true regardless of lesbians' original mothering desires. Again the decision largely came down to finding the right partner at the right time. The lesbians who were influenced by their partners to become mothers tended to be from the middle class, suggesting that finding the right partner is a benefit of class privilege. Some of these lesbians really wanted to become mothers but did not want to parent alone. Therefore, the ability to find a partner was critical to their decision. As Grace, a middle-class White lesbian, stated:

I could not see myself having any children without having a partner, specifically my partner. But as much as I wanted kids, . . . I cannot see myself raising a child by myself.

Other lesbians were ambivalent but ultimately decided to become mothers in part because they found partners who wanted to have children. For example, Patricia, a middle-class White lesbian who was ambivalent about motherhood, stated:

I went back and forth as a young person: I was not going to
have kids ever, I would never be a good mother. And I really
didn't want kids. And I think that as I got older and I started
reaching sort of the biological clock point where it starts
the countdown and I was single for a really long time and I
thought, "Well, maybe I'll have a kid by myself." And that just
seemed like that was, it was sort of so hard that I couldn't really envision it. And then when I met my current partner she
really wanted kids. And it was clear in her mind that she had
never been in a relationship where she felt like that was a solid
enough relationship, and stable enough too, to do that. We've
been together now nine years, and when we first got together,
probably within the first six or eight months, we started talking
about that concept and that if we stayed together, [having kids]
was something we wanted to do.

As Patricia's story shows, for her, meeting the right person at the right
time was critical to her decision. For her, having the "right" partner
meant being in a solid relationship. Similarly, the "right" time was
when she realized that biologically she did not have much more time
to decide. Their decision and "good fit" as partners was eased by the
fact that she and her partner both benefited from economic stability
afforded by their middle-class status.

Like Patricia, other lesbians who were ambivalent about motherhood also found partners who encouraged them to have children. For
example, Miriam, a middle-class Black lesbian who always expected to
remain childfree, explained:

I always liked kids and without thinking it consciously, I think
I just thought maybe I would never have any, or maybe I would
hook up with someone who already had some and that would
be cool. But . . . I never considered being a mother until my
partner brought it up. That's the first time I really thought
about it: "Do I want it or not?"

As I discuss in chapter 8, Miriam was in a job she disliked and Desiree was tired of going to law school. The combination of declining

work aspirations and an encouraging partner were two factors that Miriam weighed heavily in her decision to become a mother, despite her earlier thoughts that she would remain childfree.

Carly, a middle-class White lesbian, was also ambivalent about motherhood before she met her partner. When she was younger, Carly had given up the thought of becoming a mother because she did not think lesbians could have children. Not only did her partner persuade her otherwise, but her partner's desire to have children was a driving force in Carly's decision to become a mother:

> We decided to get married. And in that process we went through a lot of thinking about our likes and dislikes and what we had in common and what we didn't have in common [and] discovered that we both wanted kids. And I think that [my partner] wanted kids more than I did. I think about it now, and I think that I kind of just went along. And I was perfectly happy with it, don't get me wrong about that, [but] I don't think that I would ever have had kids if I didn't have a partner [who wanted them].

Like Miriam, Carly was happy with her mothering decision. However, it is likely that both of them, as well as other lesbians in the study, would have remained childfree had they been partnered with a woman who did not want children.

Whereas both Carly's and Miriam's partners directly influenced their decisions to become mothers by discussing children and agreeing to co-mother, Janet, a working-class White lesbian, described how her partner indirectly—but very strongly—influenced her decision to become a mother. Janet's partner had already decided to become a mother before Janet and she got together. Her partner did not try to persuade Janet to become a mother. Rather, it was the bond between Janet's partner and her infant son that led Janet to decide to become a mother:

> JANET: [My partner and I] had been really close friends prior to our becoming partners . . . I always thought there would be children in my life, I just didn't realize that I was going to

deliver one. Like I said, [my partner] had already started the process. She had already been through two or three inseminations and had been unsuccessful. When we got together she took a few months off and started up again, and it was two more tries and she was pregnant, so our relationship, we had only been in it six months when she got pregnant.

NM: So you hadn't necessarily thought about actually becoming a mother before you and your partner got together?

JANET: No, not at all. Nope. I just knew we were going to be partners, and she was going to have a kid, and I was going to help raise it, and it wasn't until after we had a child that I realized there's a lot more to this than just hanging out in the hospital holding her hand while she screams her guts out [laughs] and delivers that big-headed baby. I never wanted to do it myself . . . I was ambivalent, I think, is probably the best way to describe it . . . I wouldn't do it by myself as a choice. There's no way I would choose to be a parent alone. The one biggest deciding factor for me was . . . my partner having the first child and not feeling close the way I wanted to. It was almost immediate, [my partner and her son's] bond. And it was obvious. Even though I loved him—I loved him a lot—but when he was in distress or upset, he wanted her. And I didn't handle that well at first at all. I didn't like it at all. But like I said, after a year or two of that I realized that maybe I just don't know what to do, or how to do it, or how it feels, and so I thought I would try. And there wasn't even a concerted effort. It was just, "Well, I'm going to try this. If it happens, it happens. And if not, wham, it wasn't meant to happen. Yep, I don't care if it happens." Which was a lie, 'cause I cared a lot . . . That was the biggest issue for me to make the decision to try and do it myself, was wanting to feel close to my first one, and believing that doing it myself would teach me. And I lucked out and was right. [laughs] . . . And I don't know if I even considered myself a true parent until then, to be honest, which is my prejudice, I guess. You know, I never knew people that were adopted. It was out of my experience, completely out of my experience.

In addition to explaining the significant effect partners can have on mothering decisions, Janet's experience also illustrates the importance some lesbians place on the biological connection between mother and child. Janet did not consider herself to be a true parent to the first child because she had not birthed him. Furthermore, she so strongly attributed to biology the bond her partner had with her son that Janet wanted to recreate that bond with her own biological child. She thought that having such a bond would make her a better parent to her partner's son, which she said it did. Other lesbians in the study, particularly ones who adopted or who had infertility problems, did not place such a strong emphasis on biological connections between mother and child. Regardless of personal beliefs about what bonds parents and children, Janet's story illustrates the various ways in which intimate partners figure in mothering decisions.

WHEN PARTNERS JUST DON'T MATTER

For most lesbians, partners were a major consideration in making mothering decisions. But several lesbians in the study made their decisions regardless of their partner status. When they weighed the prospect of a partner against their desires to remain childfree or to mother, they found that their desires outweighed their need for a partner; or they specifically chose partners who held similar mothering desires. Lily, a middle-class White lesbian who always wanted to become a mother, explained that if she ever dated a woman who did not want to have children, that woman was not an eligible life partner. When she and her partner were deciding to move in together, Lily said:

> It was the make-or-break question to me: "Well, if [having children] is okay, then we'll get together. Otherwise, no."

Lily would have left her partner if her partner had said she did not want children.

Just as choosing a partner was a strategy for lesbians who strongly desired motherhood, it was also a strategy for lesbians who wanted to remain childfree. For some lesbians, the desire to remain childfree was so strong that they avoided relationships with women who wanted children, or they would leave a relationship because their partners wanted to have children. I found that this strategy was used particularly by White lesbians. Unlike Black lesbians such as Roxanne, Leslie, and Terry, who said they preferred not to parent but would not have left a partner had she wanted children, several White participants strongly expressed a desire to only be with a partner who wanted to remain childfree. White lesbians may have felt they could be more selective in their choice of partners because there was a larger pool of potential partners from which to choose than there was for Black lesbians. That larger pool was particularly available to middle-class White lesbians who were connected to larger lesbian communities (see chap. 6). My analysis of race differences assumes, however, that lesbians of color prefer to be partnered with other lesbians of color, an assumption that I did not explore in my research.

To illustrate White lesbians' desires to avoid relationships in which a potential partner might want children, Judy, a middle-class White lesbian, explained:

> Any time anybody I dated ever started talking about children, I ran. I should've held the TV show on Who Wants to Be a Childless Lesbian Couple? [laughter] And my current partner feels pretty much the same way, too, very much the same way. She runs from the room when children come in.

Similarly, Eve, a working-class White lesbian, explained:

> I was in a relationship for a short time, but during that time kids did come up. And I was the one who was going to get to have them, and there was a little pressure in that situation. But it was a short-term relationship, and I was out of there too fast to even have it come up again.

Both Eve and Judy made it clear that they did not want to be mothers and therefore were not willing to be partnered with someone who wanted children.

Other lesbians who were ambivalent about motherhood often

weighed a combination of factors related to intimate partner relationships in making their mothering decisions. Tammy, a middle-class White lesbian, turned away a partner who wanted to have children not solely because of the partner but because the partner wanted children before Tammy was ready to take on parenting responsibilities. On the basis of her own mother's experience, Tammy had decided that she was not going to make any mothering decision until she was 30 years old, because she wanted to be settled into a career first:

> I had always said it, watching my mom when she was married at 18 and had all her kids by 30, and there's four of us, and I had said, "No, I'm going to wait until I'm 30 to make any decision whether to have children or not" . . . I guess I had said I'm going to [have] a career first, and I'm going to be settled in a career 'cause, going back to what I had mentioned earlier, I watched my mom raise all these children and not—I mean, she tried to go back to college and wasn't able to do it 'cause there was just too many kids at home.

When I asked Tammy about how intimate partners factored into her decision to remain childfree, she told me that she had a previous partner who wanted children. I asked her why she was no longer with that partner. She responded:

> Why I'm not with that person? Um, she really wanted to have children. She wanted me to have children, and I was like, "Ohhhh noooo" [laughter] . . . And I discussed with her that my thought was, "Oh no, I have to have a career first. I'm not going to sacrifice that." And then at 30 and [the relationship] just wasn't working and I moved on. I'm with a partner now who, I think she would probably go either way with whether we had a child or not, but is happy with not having a child. We love to go on vacation; we like to get up and just go. And you can't really do that . . . with a child.

Tammy's story illustrates how lesbians often weigh several factors in making their mothering decisions. Tammy was ambivalent about motherhood because of what she saw her mother go through. She knew she wanted to have a career and wasn't so sure she wanted to have children. When push came to shove with a partner who wanted to have children, Tammy chose a career over both the partner and motherhood. As she continued to live a childfree life, even with a partner who would have considered children, she realized that there were many advantages to remaining childfree. Her middle-class status, partially secured by her choice to pursue a career instead of motherhood, allowed her to participate in a variety of fulfilling activities. So after she made her decision to remain childfree, like most other childfree lesbians I interviewed, she felt good about the decision. In talking about leaving her partner who wanted children and focusing on her career, Tammy said:

> It was a big life change to make that switch, but I'm comfortable. After I got to that point I said, "Oh, this is right."

While some lesbians decided to forgo partners, or choose their partners carefully, in order to remain childfree, two lesbians I interviewed said they always wanted to become mothers and made conscious decisions to be single mothers, choosing motherhood over partners. Both single parents, Anita and Rita, were middle-class. Anita was Latina and Rita was White. Class privilege was key to their decisions, as both were financially able to support children without a second income. As Anita explained, she was partnered at the time when she adopted her first child. However, that relationship did not last, mostly because her partner did not want children:

> I had been in this relationship for seven years, and for a couple of years we had talked about, or I had talked about, wanting to have a child, and it was like, "No, no, no, no." And it just—you know, I would make agreements: "Okay, I'll wait a year, and then we'll talk about it again." Well, it was always the same, so I went ahead. And once I decided to look into adoption, I went ahead and did that, and I actually had [that child] for several months, almost a year, in that relationship, and it wasn't working out. It was definitely single parenting, trying to make this relationship work, and what became more important to me was

parenting, being a mom, and I remember saying—I remember the corner we were on as I said this—"I'm ready for another child." And she said, "Well, you better find another girlfriend." And I said, "Okay," and that was pretty much it.

Although Anita was a single mother for a while, she later met a woman with whom she was partnered at the time of the interview. Anita's partner had her own grown children but was willing to co-mother the four children Anita had adopted. Even though Anita ultimately ended up with support and help from an intimate partner, she did not have that kind of support while making the decision to become a mother. Anita was willing to end a seven-year relationship in order to become a mother.

Whereas Anita left a partner to become a mother, Rita, a middle-class White lesbian, decided not to wait to be partnered before having children because she thought it might never happen. As she explained, she did not want to fall into the trap of not finding the "right" person at the "right" time, so she chose not to be bothered with looking:

> I had always thought I wanted to have kids. And I thought I'd be in a relationship before I did it. But when I went through my last breakup I couldn't see how I was going to get involved with somebody and have enough time to have that be stable and then— and then have kids at a time in my life where I felt comfortable with it.

Rita would have preferred to parent with a partner. But she said that given her history of relationships and how much energy they took to maintain, she found there is an advantage to being single. Not only could she put all her energy into her child, but she could make her own parenting decisions, thus avoiding the arguments around child-rearing practices that can arise in two-parent relationships.

Although Anita and Rita did not receive support from an intimate partner, their middle-class status gave them access to other forms of support, thus enabling them to become single mothers. In particular, both were well integrated into formal lesbian mother support networks. Furthermore, both were able to rely on the benefits of work (e.g., stable, flexible jobs with good incomes) to compensate for the lack of support from another factor (intimate partners) in deciding to become mothers. Like many of the lesbians in my study, Anita and Rita weighed multiple factors in making their mothering decisions. Ultimately they chose motherhood over partners.

FINDING THE RIGHT PARTNER AT THE RIGHT TIME

As the preceding discussion suggests, intimate partner relationships were an important factor that lesbians weighed in their decisions to become mothers or remain childfree. Not finding the right partner at the right time could encourage lesbians who wanted to become mothers, or who were ambivalent about motherhood, to remain childfree. Finding the right partner at the right time could also persuade lesbians who never thought they would have children, or were not sure if they wanted to have children, to become mothers. And sometimes the desire to mother or remain childfree was so strong that no partner could change that desire into a differing mothering decision.

Class structures were key in shaping lesbians' relationships with intimate partners because they shaped how lesbians defined the "right" partner and the "right" time. The constraints posed by class meant that working-class lesbians had more criteria than their middle-class counterparts for defining "right," particularly the criterion of financial stability for both the lesbian herself and her partner at a time when both were emotionally ready for children. The constraints of class created numerous criteria, and therefore a narrow window of opportunity in which working-class lesbians could find the right partner at the right time. Conversely, the privilege of class meant that middle-class lesbians had fewer criteria, thus creating a wide window of opportunity for finding the right partner at the right time.

In addition, in the locale where I conducted my research, strong lesbian networks both of childfree lesbians and lesbian mothers were available mainly to middle-class lesbians, with some variations by race (see chap. 6). The class and race shaping of lesbian communities and support networks meant that middle-class lesbians were privileged by the availability of other lesbians from similar backgrounds. This gave them more options not only to find the right partner at the right time but also to decide to leave a partner if the partner had a differing view of motherhood. Likewise, middle-class lesbians who wanted to remain childfree could find partners who also wanted to remain childfree. The childfree Black lesbians I interviewed were more willing than their White counterparts to stay with a partner who wanted children, perhaps because it was not so easy for them to find partners in a racially discriminatory lesbian community. White lesbians were perhaps more confident about leaving a partner if they had differing ideas about remaining childfree. Similarly, White lesbians made it clear that if they wanted children, their partners had to want them too, otherwise they would look elsewhere.

Although leaving a partner is rarely an easy decision, White lesbians may have had a larger pool of lesbians from which to choose after they left their partner. In addition to increased access to lesbian support networks and potential partners, lesbians who wanted to have children regardless of a partner were able to become mothers only because of their class-privileged financial situations, which gave them access to flexible, well-paying jobs with health benefits, a point I discuss more fully in chapter 8. Class and race structures created, therefore, more options for middle-class and White lesbians in weighing intimate partner relationships than for working-class lesbians and lesbians of color.

CHAPTER EIGHT

Considering the Benefits and Barriers of Work

As the three previous chapters have shown, lesbians consider a variety of factors when making their mothering decisions. They weigh their mothering desires in relation to their personal beliefs about motherhood, the amount and kinds of support they receive from lesbian networks and communities, and their relationships to intimate partners. Many of these factors overlap with one another, thus shaping complex decision-making processes. In addition, work also overlaps with these three factors, particularly because work is partly what makes up class status (see chap. 3), and class status shapes the entire decision-making process. However, because only limited research to date has examined decision-making processes among women in general, regardless of sexual identity, we know very little about how work—separate from other factors—shapes women's mothering decisions.

Instead, much of the literature on work as it relates to motherhood looks at how mothers balance work and family *after* their children are born. Research often focuses on a multitude of factors affecting this balance, including the second shift that women do in the form of housework after they come home from a day spent in the paid labor force, how the service economy increases women's and men's need to work more, thus reducing time at home, the amount of money women lose by taking time off work to become mothers, how to find acceptable and affordable childcare, family-friendly policies at work, whether it is better for children to have mothers who stay at home or who have occupations, and a host of other concerns about how to balance work and family responsibilities (Crittenden, 2001; Gerson and Jacobs, 2004; Hochschild, 1989; Steiner; 2006). Although the research focusing on work-family balance is rich and insightful as it describes perhaps the most significant issue today facing families with children, the literature lends little insight into how women, regardless of sexual identity, decide to become mothers or remain childfree.

Because so little research has focused on the very question of how women make mothering decisions, and because the women I interviewed stressed the importance of work in their decision-making processes, it is critical to look at how work—separate from other factors—shapes the processes women go through in order to decide if they will become mothers or remain childfree. In other words, in addition to understanding how work shapes women's lives after they have children, we also need to understand how work shapes women's decisions to have children at all. This chapter describes how the lesbians I interviewed drew on the benefits and barriers of work to decide to become mothers or remain childfree, and how those benefits and barriers varied by race and class.

The little information we do currently have on work's influence on mothering decisions pertains exclusively to heterosexual women and shows how heterosexual women draw on the benefits and barriers of work to help them achieve their personal goals, including their mothering desires. In some cases, heterosexual women take into consideration the balance between work and family responsibilities in their decisions to become mothers or remain childfree. For example, for middle- and working-class White heterosexual women, the lure of a career is the single greatest factor drawing women *away* from motherhood (Faux, 1984). Rising work aspirations and expanding work opportunities allow women to explore interests outside of domestic ones (Bartlett, 1994; Faux, 1984; Gerson, 1985; Ireland, 1993). In addition, both middle- and working-class women may find it difficult to fit children into their work schedules, although the reasons vary by class. For middle-class college-educated women, careers mean not only upward mobility but also a degree of job satisfaction that allows them to expand upon educational and professional interests. In contrast, many working-class women choose work over motherhood for the chance to move ahead financially (Gerson, 1985; Morell, 1993).

Contrary to the ways in which work encourages White heterosexual women to remain childfree, *declining* work aspirations due to blocked mobility and dead-end careers often lead heterosexual women into motherhood (Gerson, 1985). Even a heterosexual woman who "harbors deep-seated ambivalence toward mothering and domesticity but over time experiences *falling work aspirations*" will move toward motherhood (Gerson, 1985, p. 19). In other words, when work offers few benefits in terms of upward mobility or personal fulfillment, motherhood becomes more attractive than work. However, for all women, regardless of sexuality, the option to leave the workplace and to move into a primarily domestic role is a privilege of class because it requires that there be a second income large enough to support the family.

Although there is some information about lesbians' general experiences at work (Rasi and Rodriquez-Nogues, 1995; Reimann, 2001; Sullivan, 2004), we know virtually nothing about how work shapes their mothering decisions. My research shows that, like heterosexual women, lesbians draw on the benefits and barriers of work to help them decide how to achieve their personal goals, including goals related to motherhood. In addition, lesbians take into consideration their understanding of the relation between work and family responsibilities to help them decide to become mothers or remain childfree. However, because of how sexuality and gender intersect with race and class to shape the institution of work, how work shapes lesbians' decision-making processes varies in important ways from the experiences of heterosexual women.

HOW WORK ENCOURAGES LESBIANS TO
REMAIN CHILDFREE

Among the lesbians in my study, work encouraged some of them to remain childfree, both by providing benefits to those who wanted to achieve personal goals outside of motherhood and also by imposing constraints that encouraged lesbians who wanted to become mothers to ultimately decide to remain childfree. More specifically, work encouraged lesbians to remain childfree in two major ways. First, work helped lesbians to achieve upward mobility or to maintain their current economic status. Second, by denying some lesbians access to health insurance and domestic partner benefits, work encouraged some lesbians to remain childfree.

Most of the lesbians in my study actively drew on the benefits of work to help them attain personal goals, including those pertaining to mothering desires. Within every group I interviewed, lesbians discussed how they used work to address concerns about financial stability. However, there were variations in the focus of that concern, particularly by class and mothering desire. Much like heterosexual women, working-class lesbians and those from working-class backgrounds spoke primarily about how remaining childfree allowed them to achieve upward mobility. For some lesbians, work provided the material opportunity needed to achieve their goal of economic freedom, a goal many saw as being mutually exclusive with having children. Furthermore, work provided a means of reducing fears of downward mobility, which many lesbians, particularly those coming from working-class backgrounds, equated with motherhood.

For example Kristy, a middle-class White lesbian who came from a working-class background and who was ambivalent about motherhood, stated:

> I had a real strong drive to get out of my working-class background. And where I grew up was a very small town, and I wanted to get out of the small town, get out of the trap that I perceived it to be . . . And I was really driven to succeed. I'm sure that much of the reason that I moved up as far as I have so far is because I was able to make that kind of a single-minded pursuit. And I was able to keep going to school while I was doing it, and get the degrees that I've gotten. And [being driven] has made me promotable, and I don't think I could have ever done that if I'd had a family.

Other participants from working-class backgrounds voiced similar views about the inability to be upwardly mobile if also a mother. Terry, a working-class Black lesbian, stated that work greatly influenced her decision to remain childfree:

> TERRY: Right now I'm still trying to move forward, and I have one more goal to reach. Even though I have a good job, there's one place that I want to work inside of the office itself. So moving around, I don't think that's good for a child anyway, you know?

> NM: So right now your job aspirations take precedence and are more important [than becoming a mother]?

> TERRY: Yeah, yeah. They come first right now.

Whereas Kristy said that having children would be bad for her in terms of achieving upward mobility, Terry voiced her concern that having a job would be bad for a child. Regardless of the meaning they assigned to the relation between work and motherhood—and the difficulties in balancing the two—many working-class lesbians wanted to move up the financial ladder and did not see motherhood fitting into that goal. Mabel and Kerry, two working-class White lesbians, also commented on the conflict between becoming a mother and achieving personal financial goals:

> MABEL: I think when you don't have children you tend to work more, you tend to go after promotions or maybe working more, or transfers or just different things. I think your work becomes a bigger part of your life maybe than it would if you had children. So I think you either have one or the other.

> KERRY: I agree with what she was saying, because when the boys were living with us, they [took all] the time. That was where my focus needed to be at the time, and so at work I just went in and punched the clock, did my job, and went home. Well, now I'm in management, which takes up a lot more time, and I'm working towards going up the chain, and I really don't feel it would be fair . . . to any child at this point in time.

In addition to wanting to climb the economic ladder, some working-class lesbians, particularly lesbians of color, found that even if they wanted to become mothers, their jobs did not provide them with adequate financial stability to help them fulfill their desires to become mothers. A few working-class White lesbians and working-class lesbians of color stated that they had stable, well-paying jobs. However, many others said that a lack of finances was a major barrier to having children. In such cases, working-class lesbians often waited to be more financially secure before having children. Pam, a Latina who was a financially strapped graduate student from a working-class background, explained that the problem of delaying the decision to become a mother is that lesbians risk becoming too old before they become financially stable. This is particularly true for lesbians as opposed to heterosexual women, because lesbians cannot rely on a male income to support them. Because men on average earn significantly more than women (Andersen, 2006), if a working- or middle-class heterosexual woman is married, she can expect to have a household income higher than that of a lesbian and her female partner.

In explaining the events that led to her remaining childfree, Pam stated:

When you look back on it, it was really a long series of events. I mean, when I was feeling the biological pressure, which was about the time that I was 42, [it] was at the time when a lot of my friends who are little bit younger than me were like 38, 39, and said, "Bing, I have to have a child now. I am either adopting or artificial insemination." And leading up to that, at that time I was two years into a doctoral program and said, "It doesn't look like I'm going to be done anytime soon. I don't have any money. I'm not in a relationship. If I did want to have a child, as far as me biologically having a child, it's either now or never." Also because I could tell through my body changes that I'm probably [going to] go through menopause before I'm 50. And so I decided that there's enough children in my life surrounding me that I've decided that probably this just isn't gonna work out. And in some ways it's a regretful decision. You know, like if you had enough money in the world or you had

someone else to raise a child with, I think it would be something I would seriously consider. I probably wouldn't have even
thought that when I was in my 20s. In my 20s I definitely said,
"I don't want to have children." I didn't feel any biological urge.

Pam struggled with her mothering decision more than most of the
other participants who ultimately remained childfree. But Pam's discussion illustrates a few important points. First, it demonstrates how
a lack of money, as well as the lack of a partner (see chap. 7), created a
structure of constraints (Gerson, 1985) that prevented her from becoming a mother. In addition, Pam's remarks illustrate how age eventually
makes the decision for women, regardless of sexual identity (Morell,
1994). She mentioned later in the interview that she was aware that
conceptive technologies are available to older women who wish to have
children. However, she said that she would have to "win a million dollars"
before she could afford such services. And coming from a working-
class background, she most likely did not have the option of borrow-
ing money from her family of origin. A class status that created financial instability, combined with the lack of a partner at the "right" time
in Pam's life, ultimately sealed Pam's decision to remain childfree.

Like Pam, Diane, a working-class Black lesbian, delayed having
children because she could not afford them. Had it not been for finding a younger partner who wanted to become a mother, Diane's lack of
financial security might have led her to be childfree much in the same
way as it did Pam. Diane explained:

> I would not choose to have a child if I was unemployed and on
> welfare. You know, I wouldn't do that. Children are very expen-
> sive, and all your money goes to the child. And I would want
> to be able to provide everything for the child, so unless I had a
> decent job, I wouldn't do that. And in the past, if I didn't have
> a good job, I would work two and three jobs to make it up, and
> then there's no time [to raise a child]. So that's not going to
> work either, 'cause I don't want my child raised by a babysitter.
> After I started working and I went to school . . . and then my
> income was not where I thought [it was] stable enough where

I could raise a child, and I kept waiting and waiting, and time
kept going on.

Diane took into consideration how to balance work and family to the
point at which, at age 44, she thought she had lost her opportunity
to mother. However, when she and Kizzy became partners, she felt
that she had a "second chance." Because Kizzy wanted children and
was younger than Diane, Diane was hopeful that she would still become a mother. One advantage that lesbians have over heterosexual
women in similar situations is that lesbians can find younger or more
fertile partners who are able to get pregnant. Whereas older heterosexual women have the option of adopting a child or using conceptive
technologies, older lesbians have the added opportunity of becoming a
mother through younger partners.

Although working-class lesbians had deeper financial concerns
than middle-class lesbians, middle-class lesbians also discussed concerns about work and financial matters. However, they differed from
working-class lesbians in that they were less concerned about moving up the financial ladder and more concerned with maintaining
their current financial position. Not only did middle-class lesbians see
motherhood as a barrier to upward mobility, they also saw it as a cause
of downward mobility. This view was tied closely to racialized and
gendered ideas about motherhood, particularly among middle-class
White lesbians. Because many of them interpreted their own mothers'
experiences as being mutually exclusive with work (see chap. 4), and
because many of them believed that mothers should stay home with
their children, many of the middle-class White lesbians in my study
did not see how they could maintain their financial positions and still
become mothers. Andrea, a middle-class White lesbian, said that if
she were to become a mother, she would want to take time off to raise
the child. However, taking time off would compromise her and her
partner's financial stability, as she explained:

> I have the higher income of the two of us, and should I decide
> to take time off to have a child and things like that, economi-
> cally it would affect our economic status and [the] possibility for

promotions at work and things like that. So that was a factor [in my decision to remain childfree].

Andrea's comment reflects not only a fear that motherhood would prevent her from being upwardly mobile (i.e., getting promoted) but a fear that motherhood and the need to stay home would cause her and her partner to be downwardly mobile.

Many lesbians' discussion of work revealed that they used the combination of their jobs and their childfree status as a strategy to meet their personal financial goals. Lesbians from less secure financial positions within working-class backgrounds used work and being childfree as a strategy for gaining upward mobility. Middle-class lesbians, on the other hand, who came from financially secure backgrounds, used work and being childfree as a strategy for not only improving but also maintaining their financial position. As with many heterosexual women, for these lesbians their desires for economic stability outweighed their desires for motherhood. In addition, work intersected with gendered and racialized notions of motherhood to steer those lesbians (regardless of class) who viewed motherhood and work as mutually exclusive, and as hindering personal economic mobility and freedom, toward remaining childfree. In other words, work provided the necessary financial benefits to help some lesbians attain personal economic goals and therefore encouraged them to remain childfree.

Work also encouraged lesbians to remain childfree by creating a barrier to motherhood in the form of denied access to health insurance and domestic partner benefits. This was particularly true for working-class lesbians. Jobs that did not offer strong health benefits also did not offer the financial support that lesbians needed to become mothers. Because health benefits are mostly accessible through work, work deterred some of the lesbians in my study from becoming mothers because without benefits, they were unable to pay for costly conceptive technologies or to cover the medical expenses incurred after a child is born or adopted.

The lack of health insurance was important to lesbians' decisions to remain childfree because those who wanted to become mothers and have a biological connection with their children needed to access expensive conceptive technologies such as donor insemination. If they encountered any fertility issues, then additional medical services might be necessary, such as IVF. The middle-class White lesbians in my study were less concerned with insurance issues because they were more likely to hold jobs that offered such benefits. But the lack of health insurance occupied the minds of many working-class lesbians who had less secure jobs or fewer health benefits than their middle-class counterparts. When I asked working-class White lesbians if there were any resources not available to them, Amanda laughed and answered jokingly, "Excuse me, I'm sorry: the obvious one." Although here she was referring to sperm, she then added more seriously:

> As far as resources not available, I think in general [it] would be finances. I mean, we had some friends who for five years kept trying to get pregnant. This was back almost ten years ago, and the cost for each attempt of artificial insemination was $1,000.

Like Amanda, most of the lesbians in the study knew that conceptive technologies were expensive. For those without substantial savings, a large income, or help from health insurance or family members, the cost of conceptive technologies was prohibitively high.

Because of the expense, only lesbians with health benefits that covered at least some of the cost were able to use conceptive technologies, particularly when they faced serious fertility problems. As Beth, a middle-class Black lesbian, explained, both she and her partner Kathy (a middle-class White lesbian who also participated in the study) needed fertility treatments that led to the use of more expensive medical procedures. But their health insurance covered some of the cost:

> It was real interesting because we were in an HMO [and] while they will cover any of the pills [and] any of the medical tests— the HCG [hormones], the whole nine yards—they won't cover the insemination itself, which again became our own cost.

Given the health insurance coverage Beth and Kathy received through their middle-class jobs, covering the extra cost was manageable. But for working-class lesbians, not only would they have to cover the *extra* cost on a limited income, but they would also have to cover the *entire* cost because either they had no health insurance at all or the insurance did not cover conceptive technologies.

A related concern to the lack of health care benefits for working-class lesbians was the lack of domestic partner benefits. Because of heterosexist policies that prevent the instituting of same-sex marriage, civil unions, or domestic partner benefits on a federal, state, local, and private level, sharing health and other work-related benefits is not an option for most lesbian couples. Unlike many married heterosexual women whose husbands' health benefits automatically cover their families, lesbians rarely have that privilege. The lack of domestic partner benefits, coupled with the lack of health insurance, made accessing conceptive technologies nearly impossible for working-class lesbians. When working-class lesbians began considering the barriers of work, particularly in the form of a lack of health and domestic partner benefits, they often decided to remain childfree.

Frustration about the lack of domestic partner benefits was most loudly voiced by working-class White lesbians. Their frustration was compounded by their own beliefs that mothers should stay home with their children. Lack of domestic partnership benefits that could provide health insurance to the potential stay-at-home partner and the children was therefore a serious concern. For example, Clara, a working-class White lesbian who was ambivalent about motherhood, explained:

> Insurance is a big thing. If a cost is a big thing to me, then insurance would be a big thing to me. Getting partners covered on the insurance. I mean, it's all a chain reaction right there, so I would say that would be one point.

Many of the other working-class White lesbians I interviewed shared Clara's sentiment. Clara's comment that "it's all a chain reaction" indicates how sexual discrimination shapes the institution of work such that work policies and mothering decisions become closely related to one another. Most adult Americans who have health and financial benefits get them through work or their legal spouse. And most American employers do not offer domestic partner benefits. The result is that many working-class lesbians may not have access to health insurance through their work and cannot be covered by their partner's health insurance. Without the economic ability to finance conceptive technologies on their own, working-class lesbians found that economic barriers created through work thwarted their personal desires to become mothers. As Amanda, a working-class White lesbian, explained about her and her partner:

> For the majority of ten years one or the other of us has not had insurance, and that's been a medical drawback and a big financial drawback.

So for working-class lesbians with limited finances and jobs without domestic partner benefits, the lack of benefits and the economic strain that may follow because of medical expenses become a huge barrier that ultimately led many working-class lesbians to remain childfree.

But for working-class lesbians, heterosexism and homophobia may run deeper than just a lack of domestic partner benefits. Not only did many working-class jobs lack domestic partner benefits, but my study suggests that working-class lesbians may be reluctant to take advantage of such benefits even when they are offered. Kerry was the only working-class lesbian in my study who said her partner's job offered domestic partner benefits. When she shared this information with the others in the focus group, they all responded with surprise: "Wow! Really?!" Kerry said, however, that she could not persuade her partner to fill out the necessary paperwork to activate the benefits. Just as I found it difficult to recruit working-class lesbians to participate in my study for fear that they would be "outed," Kerry's experience suggests that some working-class lesbians are wary of taking advantage of domestic partner benefits for fear of "outing" themselves at work, an act they believe could cost them their jobs. With only a handful of state and local governments protecting them against sexual discrimination, lesbians and gays have little or no legal recourse once fired. Thus, for lesbians whose financial survival fully depends on their ability to work, and who have few job skills or little educational collateral on which to rely, the risk of losing a job often outweighs the advantages of accessing domestic partner benefits. The intersection of class structures (in the form of limited financial security among the working class) with sexual structures (in the form of sexual discrimination of lesbians) means that work presents different barriers to lesbians than to heterosexual women, barriers that often led the working-class lesbians in my study to remain childfree.

HOW WORK ENCOURAGES LESBIANS TO BECOME MOTHERS

While the benefits that work offered in helping lesbians attain personal economic goals, and the barriers that work created through a lack of health and domestic partner benefits, encouraged some lesbians to remain childfree, work also presented benefits and barriers that led mostly middle-class lesbians to become mothers. When middle-class lesbians, regardless of race, considered their personal goals in relation to work, they found that work presented them with a variety of options. Their options derived from the fact that many of them were able to achieve their personal career and financial goals early enough in their lives that they still had time to become mothers if they so desired. As with heterosexual women, the class privilege of the middle-class lesbians in my study allowed them to find job satisfaction and achieve financial security through their jobs. Achieving their career goals through middle-class positions provided lesbians with the benefit of having the financial security and flexibility they needed or wanted in order to become mothers.

For example, Beth, a middle-class Black lesbian, explained:

Kathy and I have been together for quite a while, so we both were career folks, and we had kids later in life. Kathy was 30 when the twins were born and I was 40 when our third child was born, so we were in a much different place. Work was never an issue 'cause again later we were both older, we were both already in career paths, and the jobs just flexed with the kids.

Beth and Kathy both had established careers and secure, flexible jobs, which gave them the option of having children without making any significant personal and economic sacrifices. Because of their middle-class privilege, work provided them with secure jobs and finances that supported and reinforced their desires to become mothers.

Also in contrast to working-class lesbians, the privilege of their job status gave middle-class lesbians the option to change how they perceived the relation between work and motherhood. June, a middle-class White lesbian who "had always sworn up and down that [she] would not be a mother," explained that once she and her partner achieved their career aspirations, they were not only financially secure but were also willing to put their careers "on the back burner." Middle-class privilege allowed June to quit her preferred job and take a more flexible job working from home. She explained that job flexibility was central to her decision to become a mother:

> I think the fact that we're both in our mid-40s, and at a point where our careers, we've kind of been there, done that. We've both gone to school and both have pretty decent jobs, and have obtained some goals that we probably wanted to do twenty years ago. The fact that we're more financially secure than we were twenty years ago, it just makes life a lot easier. And I do think it had a lot to do with [our decision]. I mean, ten years ago we wouldn't have been able to do it probably financially, and so I think it's really helped. I personally was working at the university, and when I knew that we were starting to look at adoption, I quit my job and I took a job where I could work from home. It's not a great job, and I never would have done it if I wasn't gonna have a child, but it's definitely rearranged our priorities. And the jobs are, obviously, they're secondary to anything else now . . . My partner's very career-minded. I even think that her career has been really put on the back burner since we had a child, and Lord knows mine has. And I do think that especially at this age and being able to kinda say, "Well, you know, we're not still in graduate school, we're not still working crazy hours, and we're not still trying to make ends meet so much," really, really had a lot of effect on us.

June's story shows how she weighed concerns about how to balance work and family in her decision to become a mother. In addition, because June and her partner had already achieved their desired career aspirations and had established financial security, they were able to consider motherhood later in life and were willing to make a change in their careers because they had already "been there, done that." Furthermore, because her middle-class status had already privileged June with a solid, established, and financially secure career, being able to switch jobs from one with a rigid schedule to one with a more flexible schedule was a benefit of her job that encouraged June to become a mother.

In addition to June, other middle-class participants discussed how the benefit of job flexibility and the financial means to reduce their work hours fostered their ability to choose motherhood. Rita was a single middle-class White lesbian who decided to adopt a child. At the time of her decision she was working long hours as an accountant. Anticipating the need to balance work and motherhood, Rita looked for a job with reduced hours that would better fit with her anticipated parenting schedule:

> If I hadn't been able to find a job where I could work part-time,
> I don't think I would've made the decision [to be a mother].
> I don't think I could've been a full-time-plus working single
> mother. I just decided that. So it did make a big difference
> to me. How many hours I would work and how much stress
> there would be in the job made a big difference as to whether I
> would've even had a child.

Having a marketable job skill gave Rita and most other middle-class participants the flexibility to maintain their careers in a way that accommodated their mothering responsibilities. Being able to negotiate their careers while remaining financially stable allowed many middle-class lesbians either to pursue their desires to become mothers or, as in June's case, to develop new desires to become mothers that they would not have anticipated prior to having an established and successful career.

Like middle-class lesbians, working-class lesbians also discussed how they wanted to prioritize motherhood over work. However, the lack of the economic security and job flexibility they needed to balance motherhood and work created barriers to becoming mothers. Joy, a working-class Black lesbian, was ambivalent about motherhood. She knew that although her day job could accommodate motherhood, her evening job as a professional party giver could not, and she needed her evening job in order to maintain a comfortable income. She said that when she was ready to become a mother, she would have to give up her evening job:

> I'm a party giver here. It's going to be kind of hard to be a party giver and have a baby too, or be at the party when you're seven months pregnant or something like that. It's just, you know, striving to achieve more and knowing that to do that I may have to work two jobs. It's not going to match with . . . when you have kids. But I would give that all up and just be okay if I had children.

Joy's statement that she was willing to give up her evening job in order to have children is a sentiment that many working-class participants also expressed. However, for working-class lesbians, putting children first meant forgoing part of their income, which was not easy for most of them to do, a point many of them stressed. So although middle- and working-class lesbians shared similar *desires* to prioritize motherhood over work, class privileges that shape the institution of work made it possible for middle-class lesbians to turn desire into reality, whereas class constraints left working-class lesbians without the financial means to do so. Joy's working-class and racial position ultimately created enough barriers—in the form of limited economic security through her job, a lack of an intimate partner with whom to share mothering responsibilities, and a lack of integration into lesbian networks—to lead her to decide to remain childfree.

The working-class positions of many of the lesbians I interviewed also meant that, unlike middle-class lesbians, they had trouble finding jobs that fulfilled their career goals. Although many working-class lesbians had well-paying jobs, those jobs did not complement their career aspirations. The result was that working-class lesbians had to choose between going back to school, keeping their current jobs, and having children. Janet, a working-class White lesbian, articulated this position well:

> My partner and I both have very good jobs. I mean, they are working-class jobs. I identify as working class. We could afford to have as many children as we wanted. But school—my part-

ner had already finished her bachelor's, but I didn't. [In] my job, I had to work shift work, so it was hard to go to school working a midnight shift or a relief shift where I'm working all three shifts in a week. And I made the choice to stay at that job rather than quit and go back to school. But I always wanted to finish school.

Janet did eventually complete her associate's degree after her children were old enough to occupy themselves without constant supervision. And while Janet was able to maintain her job and become a mother, being a mother meant she had to at least temporarily decide between having children and finishing her degree. No middle-class lesbians in the study discussed making such sacrifices. They did not have to, because the jobs they held offered the benefit of being able to attain their career goals.

There is no question that both middle- and working-class lesbians made sacrifices at work in order to become mothers. But just as for heterosexual women (Gerson, 1985; Morell, 1993), work benefited middle-class lesbians by allowing them to attain career goals, be financially secure, have health benefits, and have flexible work schedules. Work created a system of barriers for working-class lesbians by not providing financial security, health benefits, flexibility, or avenues for attaining career goals. The result was that in order to fulfill their desires to mother, working-class lesbians needed to delay having a child, relied on the support of an intimate partner, or sacrificed or delayed career goals. As Janet's example suggests, some working-class lesbians (particularly those who were White) were able to negotiate work and motherhood despite the many barriers work presented. However, as Joy's example suggests, the barriers work presented discouraged some lesbians, particularly working-class lesbians of color, from deciding to become mothers. In other words, the ways in which work provided benefits that encouraged some lesbians in my study to become mothers were shaped largely by race and class.

Just as work encouraged some lesbians privileged by race or class to become mothers by providing fulfilling careers and financial stability, for some lesbians work did not hold any real personal lure or excitement. As with heterosexual women (Gerson, 1985), for lesbians

with limited work aspirations, motherhood seemed like a viable substitute, a way to fill a personal void. The lesbians in my study who had
declining work aspirations had partners who worked in professional
positions such as lawyers and physicians and therefore were able to
survive on one income.

Desiree and Miriam, a couple who both came from working-class
backgrounds, exemplified this position. Desiree, a Latina, was a law-
yer who wanted to become a mother. Miriam, a Black lesbian, always
thought she would remain childfree. As Desiree explained, they
decided to have children at a time when neither was earning much
money and Desiree was tired of being in law school:

> We had moved away from [home]. We had no friends. I was in
> law school. I hated it. Miriam had a job she hated. We're like,
> "Hmmm, what should we do? We don't have much money. We
> have health care. Hmm, don't really like people at law school.
> Let's make someone who we could really hang out with." I'm
> not kidding!

Desiree and Miriam were willing to become mothers at a time when
they were not financially secure mostly because they were tired of
their current positions and wanted to do something they felt would be
more meaningful than work or graduate school. Although they both
came from working-class backgrounds, as adults they gained class
privilege through their educations and job training. Therefore, they
were able to decide to become mothers because they had enough work
experience and educational training to give them confidence that one
of them would find a job with a large enough salary to support their
family. Both Miriam and Desiree also felt strongly that at least one
parent should stay home with their child. As Miriam explained, she
was less career-oriented and did not have a job, so they decided she
would be the stay-at-home parent:

> I didn't know what I wanted to do, so it didn't really—I mean,
> I guess that helped the decision a little 'cause I knew that I
> wasn't going to [have], like, some powerful career or some-
> thing. So if you're thinking about kids getting in the way of

your career, I wasn't really a career-minded person. I guess that would've helped the decision or probably decided differently had I been.

Miriam acknowledged that her lack of job aspirations affected her decision to become a mother. Desiree was more career-oriented and wanted to pursue her opportunities as an attorney. The combination of educational training for both of them, career opportunities for Desiree, and a lack of career aspirations for Miriam granted them enough financial stability to raise their child and have one parent stay home. The few other stay-at-home mothers interviewed in the study reported a similar experience. As discussed in chapter 4, Carly, a middle-class White lesbian, had little job experience and few career aspirations, so she stayed home while her physician partner earned their income. Several lesbians who ultimately decided to remain childfree mentioned that they would have considered motherhood if they and their partner had been able to afford to have one parent stay home with their children.

THE BENEFITS AND BARRIERS OF WORK

My research shows that, like support networks and intimate partners, work creates a system of support and constraints that shape different groups of lesbians' mothering decisions in different ways. When examining how lesbians consider the benefits and barriers of work in making their mothering decisions, it becomes clear that class and race privilege shape those benefits and barriers. For middle-class lesbians, and particularly middle-class White lesbians, work provided a variety of options that ultimately supported their mothering decisions. Middle-class White lesbians could decide to remain childfree and have work support their economic and personal career goals. They could decide to become mothers and have work provide the necessary financial security, career satisfaction, flexible schedules, ability to switch jobs, and health insurance needed to balance work and motherhood on one or two women's incomes. Although there were not many differences among middle-class White lesbians and middle-class lesbians of color, middle-class lesbians of color voiced greater concern about health insurance, suggesting that their jobs did not offer this benefit as readily as the jobs held by their White counterparts.

For working-class lesbians, the options work provided were very narrow. Working-class lesbians had limited financial security and relied on their jobs to provide upward mobility. Their jobs had little flexibility, offered limited career satisfaction, and forced working-class lesbians to choose between a job, education, and motherhood. Working-class jobs also lacked adequate health insurance and domestic partner benefits. These barriers concerned working-class lesbians, regardless of race. However, whereas working-class White lesbians voiced their frustration with not having good health insurance and domestic partner benefits, working-class lesbians of color most strongly voiced their concern about a lack of financial stability and their limited options in terms of balancing work and motherhood. As a result, working-class lesbians of color were more likely than their White counterparts to delay motherhood, which in some cases meant not becoming mothers at all. Particularly for working-class lesbians, my findings show how structures of race and class intersect with sexuality to take away a safety net that working- and middle-class heterosexual women may enjoy through the benefits of their husbands' work that marriage automatically guarantees them.

The responses of the lesbians in my study suggest that lesbians are aware of, and take into consideration, issues concerning the need for mothers to balance work and family. Working- and middle-class lesbians who wanted to fulfill goals of economic and personal freedom—two benefits that came directly from work—often decided to remain childfree because they saw motherhood as undermining those goals. Lesbians who had established and flexible careers with adequate health benefits, or who had unfulfilling careers but economically stable partners, knew they could adequately balance their work and families, and so were inclined to become mothers. Lesbians' work situations were thus shaped by structures of race, class, gender, and sexuality, and were also a major factor that helped them decide to become mothers or remain childfree.

CHAPTER NINE

New Choices, New Families

When I set out to conduct my research, I wanted to know what makes lesbians decide to become mothers or remain childfree and how social conditions created through structures of race, class, gender, and sexuality shaped their decisions. Mine was a qualitative study, one that did not require me to have any hypotheses about what the answers to my questions might look like. But I was pretty sure when I set out to conduct my research that race, class, gender, and sexuality would matter *somehow*. I was confident that these four organizing forces would shape the material resources available to lesbians, as well as their cultural beliefs, personal experiences, and senses of self, in ways that showed patterns among similar groups of lesbians. I was confident about this because the research sociologists have conducted to date suggests that race, class, gender, and sexuality shape every aspect of people's personal lives. Why would mothering decisions be different? Indeed, mothering decisions are not. This chapter provides a summary of my findings, reexamines the discussion concerning intentional decision making, and looks at what we can learn from lesbians' decisions to become mothers or remain childfree. In doing so, the chapter explains how lesbians are drawing on new opportunities to create new families and how these families inform the larger study of American families in general.

SUMMARY OF FINDINGS

Speaking of motherhood, as I was writing this book, my own mother asked me for an executive summary of my research that she could share with her friends and colleagues. Shortly after that, over Thanksgiving, my father asked me, "If you could give me your one big finding, what would it be?" In an attempt to satisfy both my parents' requests, I answered, "Lesbians' mothering decisions are shaped and vary by race, class, gender, and sexuality." "Okay," my folks responded, "but how? And how can you say that what you found is specific to lesbians and not general to all women?" As I had this conversation with my parents, it occurred to me that people reading this book might have similar questions. How convenient for me, at a time when I was struggling to write this last chapter, that I now had something to write!

Although my intention has never been to conduct a comparative study between lesbians and heterosexual women, in order to understand how sexuality shapes mothering decisions, I needed to make some comparisons. In truth, I did not find major differences between how girls who later identify as lesbians develop mothering desires compared with those who later identify as heterosexual. Girls in general interpret their mothers' experiences, examine their own experiences, look around them to see what others in society are doing, and filter cultural norms about gender roles in families to figure out if mothering is something they want to do, do not want to do, or are unsure about. If my research is at all reliable, we can see that there are more similarities between how lesbians and heterosexuals develop their mothering desires than there are differences.

That said, my study shows that different mothering desires develop more on the basis of race and class than on the basis of sexuality. This is because the gendered experiences and sexual messages through which girls filter their lives are very similar both for girls who later come out as lesbians and those who identify as heterosexual. The one exception to this may be for girls who identify as lesbians at early ages. Otherwise there is little reason to think that girls who ultimately identify as lesbians would follow a different process for developing mothering desires from girls who ultimately identify as heterosexual.

Once lesbians develop their mothering desires, and as they continue on in life, I found they weigh four factors that challenge and twist, and at times change, their earlier desires. Three of the factors I identified—beliefs about motherhood, intimate partners, and work—are factors that heterosexual women consider as well. However, the substance of those factors, and how those factors shape mothering decisions, differs greatly for lesbians and heterosexual women because of how sexuality intersects with race, class, and gender to shape belief systems, intimate partner relationships, and women's relationships to work. The one remaining factor—lesbian support networks and communities—is specific to lesbians and is not a factor that heterosexual women need to consider in making their mothering decisions.

So how, in a nutshell, do these four factors shape lesbians' mothering decisions, and how do they vary by race, class, gender, and sexuality? For starters, beliefs about motherhood weighed heavily on lesbians' minds. Like heterosexual women, the lesbians in my study internalized society's beliefs about what makes a "good" mother and who should and should not become mothers. Such beliefs led some lesbians away from, and others toward, motherhood. Much like childfree heterosexual women (Bartlett, 1994; Veevers, 1980), many of the lesbians in my study discussed their aversion to pregnancy and childbirth. White lesbians in particular said that they never wanted to get pregnant. As a group, lesbians of color were equally averse to adoption. Lesbians rejected both of these options for a variety of reasons, not the least of which was the financial cost. This was particularly true for working-class lesbians, who often lacked health benefits.

Some childfree lesbians also questioned whether lesbian mothers are really different from heterosexual mothers. In addition, they questioned whether lesbian mothers understand the responsibility of motherhood or if they simply want to gain heterosexual privilege. And still other childfree lesbians had internalized the sexual discrimination they had experienced to the point of holding negative feelings about themselves and motherhood. Several working-class White lesbians also saw the world as too harsh a place in which to raise children.

In contrast, however, both lesbian mothers and childfree lesbians believed lesbian mothers to be emotionally strong, positively changing the definition of motherhood, having flexible roles within families, and teaching their children to be open-minded. Many middle-class White lesbians found that their lesbian relationships were egalitarian and flexible, offering them the chance to simultaneously be in a satisfying relationship and pursue personal goals. Being in lesbian relationships and seeing how lesbian mothers operate allowed some middle-class lesbians to reconsider their previously held negative views of motherhood. Middle-class lesbians of color also saw that lesbian relationships created space for them to become mothers because they could maintain the same sense of power and responsibility that their own mothers had manifested in their families of origin.

In addition to beliefs about motherhood, lesbians also looked to family and communities for support in making their mothering decisions. Although support networks are important to heterosexual women, because these women do not have to come out to their families, much of the substance of decision-making processes that lesbians discussed varied greatly by sexuality, as well as by race and class. Childfree heterosexual women, single heterosexual women who want to become mothers, and infertile or subfertile married heterosexual women often look to other such women for support (Cain, 2001; Hertz, 2006). However, unlike lesbians, these women do not need to reveal their sexual identities, or fear revealing their identities, in order to receive such support.

As a strategy to address sexual discrimination in larger social contexts, lesbians create social networks and communities to support their personal needs. However, the nature of these communities and access to the support they offer vary by race and class. Middle-class lesbians, regardless of race, had more access to, and flexibility within, lesbian communities. There was a friendly division between, and equally friendly mixing of, middle-class childfree lesbians and lesbian mothers. But working-class White lesbians found a hostile division between these two groups, thus limiting the support other lesbians could provide them. Working-class lesbians of color drew on a variety of support networks but had a hard time finding other lesbian mothers who might help them negotiate the medical and legal challenges to becoming mothers.

As with heterosexual women, intimate partners were also a strong factor that lesbians weighed in making their mothering decisions. For lesbians who wanted to become mothers, finding the right partner at the right time was key to whether or not they actually became mothers. However, it was easier for middle-class and White lesbians to find the "right" partner because there was a larger White lesbian community than there was for Black and Latina lesbians. In addition, the "right" partner for middle-class lesbians meant someone who wanted children and could help create a stable and loving environment. Working-class lesbians had the added criterion of finding someone who was financially stable. Having stricter requirements for a partner and fewer lesbians to choose from, working-class lesbians and lesbians of color had a more difficult time than White lesbians in finding the right partner at the right time. With few exceptions, middle-class lesbians were able to find the right partner at the right time to support their mothering desires. Furthermore, unlike heterosexual Black women, who often feel that they do not need stable partners in order to successfully mother their children (Blum and Deussen, 1996), the Black lesbians I interviewed felt that having a partner was critical to becoming a mother, largely because they wanted the financial and emotional support from a partner to help them overcome the barriers that lesbian mothers might face. For those lesbians who wanted to become mothers but did not have partners, only middle-class lesbians were able to actually become mothers. Working-class lesbians, regardless of race, in similar situations decided to forgo motherhood.

In addition to the other factors, work offers women, regardless of sexuality, the opportunity to improve and maintain their class positions. In this way, work provides an incentive, particularly for working-class women, to prioritize work over motherhood. Similarly, for both lesbians and heterosexual women with race and class privilege, work provides a variety of opportunities by allowing such women to attain career goals, be financially secure, and have flexible work schedules (Gerson, 1985; Morell, 1993). Additionally, work can encourage both lesbians and heterosexual women to become mothers when their work is in the form of a dead-end job.

Short of these three similarities, sexuality shapes lesbians' and heterosexual women's work experiences differently. My study suggests that this is true because lesbians considering motherhood often need the help of physicians for donor insemination. Because donor insemination is expensive, health benefits are particularly important. In my study, lesbians who were privileged by race and class were likely to have jobs with adequate health insurance and domestic partner benefits. This allowed both partners access to health care and gave lesbians the option to get pregnant. Because heterosexual women do not necessarily need to access conceptive technologies to get pregnant, having health insurance that covers such procedures is less important for them than for lesbians. The possible exception to this, however, includes single heterosexual women, older heterosexual women, and heterosexual women with fertility problems.

Different lesbians in my study weighed some factors more heavily than others. But for most lesbians, all four factors combined to shape their mothering decisions. Lesbians filtered their own mothering desires through the various factors in order to make their final mothering decisions. In many ways, lesbians made mothering decisions based on their beliefs about motherhood, how they could access and fit into lesbian networks and communities, their intimate partner relationships, and their relations to work. Lesbians' decision-making processes differed from heterosexual women's precisely because sexuality shapes the lives of different groups of women in different ways. But among lesbians themselves, race and class shape the lives of different groups of lesbians in different ways as well.

BETWEEN INEVITABILITY AND FREE WILL REVISITED

Given my findings, what can I say about lesbians' intentional decision making? As a sociologist I am always wary of the notion that people truly have free will. If free will is the ability to make decisions without any outside influence, decisions based solely on personal desires and capabilities, then, sociology tells us, free will is an illusion. We all exist within a particular social and cultural context. Although I don't deny the existence of individual temperaments and I understand the importance of the biological processes that make people exist and function, those temperaments and biology are only the beginning of what makes us who we are. We give so much meaning to biology that we forget that who we are comes more from the social, economic, and cultural worlds outside of us than from the hard-wiring that is inside (Johnson, 1997).

Sociologists have spent years studying how people organize society around inequalities of race, class, gender, and sexuality. Historically and currently we have divided up society by skin color, socioeconomic status, genitalia, and sexual behavior in order to figure out who gets access to rewards and resources—such as education, jobs, safe neighborhoods, leisure time, political processes, housing—and who does not. Based on this divvying up of resources, different groups of people have developed different cultural beliefs, values, attitudes, and norms to help them justify and negotiate the social positions that the structures of race, class, gender, and sexuality have created for them.

As my earlier summary of findings suggests—indeed, what this entire book suggests—is that lesbians, like all women, make their mothering decisions on the basis of their particular social and cultural contexts, regardless of what their "biological clocks" are telling them. Differences between lesbians exist because lesbians' experiences are shaped in relation to the racial, class, gendered, and sexualized conditions of their lives. As my findings demonstrate, the complex relationship between work, leisure time, income, health insurance, and access to sperm and reproductive technologies makes motherhood less of an option for some lesbians than for others. Therefore, lesbians' mothering decisions are based on an interaction between experiences outside lesbians' control and their desire and ability to take control of those experiences as best they can.

I propose that a main reason why previous research has focused on the intentional nature of lesbians' mothering decisions is that the research focused on middle-class White lesbians who have a variety of work options, health insurance, and support networks. However, although lesbians ultimately make the decision to mother or remain childfree, the more barriers they face, the harder those decisions become, particularly if they are ambivalent about motherhood or if they want to become mothers. Lesbians who are not privileged by race and class have more barriers and therefore limited options in making mothering decisions. Lesbians who are privileged by race and class have fewer barriers and more choices regarding the redefining of gender and sexual ideology, coming out, lesbian networks, intimate partners, and work, and therefore have more freedom in making their mothering decisions. In addition, the consequences of risk-taking are greater for disadvantaged lesbians than for privileged ones. So even though working-class lesbians and lesbians of color have some limited options, exercising those options is riskier for them than for middle-class and White lesbians.

The research presented in this book supports my claim that privilege facilitates intentional decision making, particularly regarding the choice to become a mother. It is not difficult for lesbians to remain childfree because there is little effort involved. There may be growing social pressure among lesbians to become mothers, but because it requires a conscious effort to become pregnant or adopt a child, remaining childfree remains the easiest path for lesbians to take.

Of the eleven participants who developed ambivalent mothering desires, only two decided to become mothers; the remaining nine decided to remain childfree. This finding suggests that ambivalence toward motherhood more often than not leads to remaining childfree. This is largely because there are many social and physical barriers standing in the way of lesbians becoming mothers. The two ambivalent lesbians in my study who decided to become mothers—Carly and Patricia—were both middle-class White lesbians. Both made their decisions largely because they had partners who wanted to become mothers and had the economic means to pay for conceptive technologies. Carly was not on any particular career path, and her partner had an income as a physician that allowed Carly to be a stay-at-home mother. Patricia also become a mother largely because of her partner. Both she and her partner had good jobs, had access to a well-organized lesbian mother network, and were economically stable enough to afford the cost of bearing and raising a child. Patricia decided to become a mother once she realized that she could have a career and be able to raise her children with a supportive partner willing to share parenting responsibilities and with other lesbian families around for additional support.

Of the eleven participants who wanted to become mothers, eight actually became mothers. At the time of the interview, Kizzy and Diane were beginning the process of becoming mothers. Six years after I originally interviewed them, they still wanted to become mothers but had not yet attained that goal. Martha and Sadie both became mothers through adopting the child of a relative or close friend who could not, or did not want, to take care of the child herself. Barb is the only middle-class lesbian who wanted to become a mother but did not. These findings suggest that many lesbians who want to become mothers can in fact do so. However, middle-class privilege facilitates their decisions.

Of the thirteen participants who wanted to remain childfree, nine actually did so while four ultimately became mothers. Janet and Miriam decided to mother because they met partners who wanted children. Kathy became a mother after she realized there were reproductive technologies that would allow her to have a biologically connected child. Being adopted herself, she felt it was important to have a biological connection with her children. June decided to become a mother after establishing her career and realizing that as a lesbian, she could have a meaningful job and redefine what being a mother is within a lesbian relationship. Pam's story differs from that of the other childfree lesbians. She stated that in her 20s and 30s, she never wanted to have children. However, somewhere around age 40, she said she "heard her eggs talking to her" and had an overwhelming biological urge to become a mother. The lack of both financial means and a partner prevented Pam from becoming a mother. But Pam's story shows that early desires and even biological urges can twist and turn and change over time. Sometimes that change leads to a new decision. In Pam's case, the twisting path led her back to her original desire, but not the desire she had later in life. Ultimately, social reasoning overpowered biological urges.

In analyzing how desires turn into decisions, I found that approximately two-thirds of the lesbians who either wanted to remain childfree or become mothers actually were able to turn their desires into corresponding decisions. However, doing so was certainly easier and more likely for lesbians privileged along lines of race and class.

In contrast to my research, Gerson's (1985) research on heterosexual women found that mothering desires, or what she calls "orientations toward motherhood," are not good predictors of mothering decisions. Why is it that the lesbians in my study were more likely than heterosexual women to achieve their desired mothering goal? I argue that the answer to this question lies precisely in how sexuality structures women's lives. Although there is pressure today from within lesbian communities for lesbians to have children, pronatalist pressure is not nearly as strong for lesbians as it is for heterosexual women. Furthermore, unless they are engaging in occasional heterosexual relationships, lesbians who want to remain childfree have little opportunity to get pregnant. Because of the absence of accidental pregnancies, for lesbians to become mothers there has to be some compelling force(s), as there were for Carly and Patricia. By the end of the 1990s, when I conducted my research, and even more so today, if lesbians have flexible and secure enough jobs, supportive partners, and social support from families of origin or lesbian mother support networks, then at this historical moment, they are often able to become mothers if they so desire. For those who really want to become mothers, if they benefit from class and race privilege, most of them can achieve their goal. In other words, race and class privilege allow certain lesbians to negotiate contradictory terrain not only more successfully than lesbians who are constrained but also more successfully than heterosexual women.

The more privilege that structures of race, class, gender, and sexuality confer upon women, the fewer barriers they will face, and therefore the more intentional their mothering decisions will be. Conversely, the more constraint that structures of race, class, gender, and sexuality impose upon women, the more barriers they will face, and therefore the less intentional their mothering decisions will be. In the end, then, my data suggest that intentionality is more nuanced than previous literature suggests. Just as Adrienne Rich (1993) discussed a "lesbian continuum," I put forth that there is an "intentionality continuum." Rather than a decision being fully intentional, there is a range of intentionality that falls between inevitability and free will. Motherhood as inevitable is based on several factors including a biological clock, pronatalist mandates for women to become mothers, and unplanned pregnancies. Motherhood as free will is based on the assumption that women make decisions totally free from social and cultural constraints. In looking specifically at lesbians, I argue that the mothering decisions of those privileged by race and class are more intentional, and therefore closer to free will, than the decisions made by lesbians who are constrained by race and class. However, when comparing lesbians with heterosexual women, I agree with the previous literature that lesbians' mothering decisions are more intentional, and therefore closer to free will, than those of heterosexual women. I would not be surprised if other decision-making processes also fit into an intentionality continuum—say, the decision to go to college, the decision to work at a particular job, or the decision to become involved in street crime or gangs—but that remains to be seen through empirical investigation.

LEARNING FROM LESBIANS

The fact that lesbians' mothering decisions are more intentional than heterosexual women's mothering decisions was a matter of pride for the lesbians I interviewed. Both childfree lesbians and lesbian mothers commented that, because their decisions were more of a choice than those made by heterosexual women, and because lesbian relationships are more egalitarian than heterosexual relationships, heterosexual women have a lot to learn from lesbians. Childfree lesbians in the study saw their decisions as a vehicle through which women can gain control over their lives. They thought that women in general, both lesbians and heterosexuals, should enter very cautiously and thoughtfully into motherhood, not only because it is a big responsibility but also because there are so many other ways for women to lead fulfilling lives.

Clara, a working-class White lesbian, described how heterosexuals had scorned her both for her sexual identity and for the fact that she was childfree. But she didn't see her life in that way and thought heterosexuals should think more carefully about their own decisions:

People usually condemn us [lesbians]. I've heard people say that lesbians and gays just don't want to grow up, that we want to be kids forever [and] don't want to have the responsibilities of parenthood and all that. And in some ways it may look that way. But I feel we're very intelligent, well-thought-out people who are trying not to be selfish because we feel cheated some way in life, and we're going to consider ourselves and what we want for the next person that we bear. I mean, I really resent when I hear [people say] how immature we are and that we think that life is a party. . . . [People] tell me that if you have a child, you just make it work. When you have a kid, you make ends meet. And I feel that's bull, because I'm a planner . . . I'm not being immature, and I'm not being a child, and I'm not negating responsibility. I'm thinking more thoroughly and clearly about it than what most heterosexual couples do because they're pushed into it.

Clara's comment focuses directly on what many childfree lesbians in my study expressed: lesbians are more responsible in their mothering decisions than heterosexual women because those decisions are more intentional.

Roxanne, a middle-class Black lesbian, agreed with Clara and then extended the discussion to include lesbian mothers:

I look at my friends, my lesbian friends within the last ten years who have had children in the context of a lesbian relationship, and it's a choice. You know, they made the choice to have a child. It's not, it's not that kind of obligatory, it doesn't have that same feel to it, that obligatory responsibility. You know, of course, they're responsible for taking care of the kids, but it's a choice. They're joyful about going through the process of making the decision to have the kid, and having kids, and raising the children. It feels a lot healthier to me for my friends from someone looking from the outside 'cause I'm not there on that day-to-day basis. I can't say what goes on everyday, but [laughs], but generally, I mean generally speaking, with all of the hassles that come along with children, it feels different. It feels like the definition of mothering is a choice: a loving, nurturing choice

that one makes to bring a child into the world and to nurture it.
So those are kind of the perspectives that I look at, and I think
having it be a choice, that it's not an obligation or responsibility
that you have to do this, to bring kids into the world—that, you
know, you actually give it some thought.

As Roxanne's comment suggests, the very notion that motherhood is
a choice placed lesbian motherhood in a positive light for many lesbians. As Kathy, a middle-class White lesbian, remarked:

> I mean, if you're a lesbian parent you are making a definite,
> concrete, often years of financial drain, emotional drain, deci-
> sion to become a parent, whether it's through adopting or hav-
> ing a child biologically. And I think that that's a real change
> from a lot of women's experiences, and that some women are
> threatened by that because they didn't have a choice. So I think
> that that right there kind of makes us think of motherhood as
> different, a choice. There's a choice. Wow, what a concept!

Kathy saw intentional decision-making as something that makes
lesbian motherhood attractive because it removes motherhood from
being a potentially unwanted obligation for, and therefore a source
of oppression to, women. She also thought that lesbian motherhood
can help change the meaning of motherhood from an obligation to a
choice, something from which heterosexual women would benefit.

Lily, a middle-class White lesbian, also observed that being a lesbian mother is a position that promotes positive change, which she
says heterosexual women often recognize and envy:

> LILY: I don't know if anybody else gets this, but a lot of straight
> women act like, "Wow, you guys have it all."
>
> ANOTHER PARTICIPANT: You've got a wife. *[laughter]*
>
> LILY: You know, she'll actually put the kids to bed.
>
> JUNE: She knows when the doctor's appointments are. Wow!
> *[laughter]*
>
> LILY: Exactly. I mean, they're like, "Wow, this would be so great

to have a partner who is kind of an equal and all." And I
think, I mean, [heterosexual women] want an equal partner,
but you know, you hear men all the time say, "Well, I gotta
go babysit my kids." Which is like, "Oh, how irritating. It's
your kids." But you know that people feel like, "Gosh, [lesbi-
ans] have it all." The other thing is, I think lesbians are one
of the strongest people I know. And you've got all these kids
who are being raised in that environment, and they're strong
kids. They just are. They're being encouraged to do a lot of
things and think.

Lily's conversation highlights a point that other lesbians in my study
agreed with: lesbian relationships are positive additions to the American family landscape. The lesbians in my study argued that women
in heterosexual relationships would particularly benefit from using
lesbian relationships and motherhood as a model for their own relationships and parenting.

Many of the lesbians in my study also specifically discussed how
lesbian motherhood was good for children and society in general.
They believed that lesbian families are helping children be stronger
and also more sensitive to gender issues and other issues of diversity. They also believed that lesbian mothers are helping to broaden
society's definition of *family*. Anita, a middle-class Latina, expressed
this opinion when she described how her family teaches outsiders that
lesbian-headed families are healthy and normal:

As the stereotype of a lesbian and a lesbian being a mother,
from my experience, from my family, from my community, I
think I am changing their perspective looking in. I think I'm
helping to educate them. Kind of show them that in their world,
if they were having doubts that how could I, being a lesbian,
possibly be a mom. Look at these, the values that I'd be showing my children, you know, morals, and I've pointed out to my
mom especially, because she's the one willing to talk about it in
my family. She'd say, "But how is it going to be?" She's worried
about my daughter. If that, what she sees then, that's what she's

going to become. I'm not going to teach her to become a lesbian
or to become a heterosexual. I'm teaching her how to be true
to herself, how to have self-esteem, to love herself, to love her
family, to be a good person who will function in society but be
true to herself. That's what I'm teaching her and I'm loving her,
and my mom was like, "Oh." And so I think for some people
looking in, I am changing that role. I have never believed that
it would be different, that I would be different being a lesbian,
but I think for relative people looking in on our family, I think
it is changing it.

Anita's comment shows how exposure to her family is changing other
people's beliefs about motherhood and family. She also discusses how
her mothering helps her daughter to be a better person. As Anita's
comment suggests, lesbians believe they are good mothers because
they teach their children to be emotionally strong and to be sensitive
to issues of discrimination, diversity, and inequality.

CONCLUSION

There is no question that American families have been changing
over the past several decades and that lesbian motherhood is a contributing force to that change. As Judith Stacey (1996) states, we have
moved from a "modern" to a "postmodern" family landscape, one that
is vast and diverse. Understanding the processes by which lesbians
make mothering decisions gives us some insight into why and how
our family landscape is changing because lesbian's mothering decisions fit squarely within a broader context of American families. In
fact, understanding lesbians' mothering decisions informs the larger
study of American families in three major ways.

First, as discussed above, my study shows that the decision-making
process that women, regardless of sexuality, go through to become
mothers or remain childfree is reliant largely upon social, cultural,
political, and economic factors, not on biological ones. In other words,
family formation is socially, not biologically, constructed. Examining
lesbians' decision-making processes explains how families are so-

cially constructed and encourages us to look at how additional taken-for-granted aspects of families are also socially constructed, such as family structure and household division of labor.

Second, all families form at a particular historical moment precisely because as new social, cultural, economic, political, and technological opportunities arise, people make new choices and form new types of families. We see this throughout human history. For example, family historians have documented at great length how social and economic "earthquakes" (Eitzen and Baca Zinn, 2006) such as the Industrial Revolution and the shift from a manufacturing to a service economy have changed American families (Baca Zinn and Eitzen, 2008; Coontz, 2000; Mintz and Kellogg, 1988). By studying lesbians' mothering decisions, we see that in this regard, lesbian families are no different from any other group of families. Social "earthquakes," such as the Gay Liberation Movement, feminism and the Women's Liberation Movement, the HIV/AIDS epidemic, and the increased use of reproductive and conceptive technologies, provided fertile ground for the development of lesbian families. As changing social conditions create new opportunities, lesbians—like all Americans, historically and currently—have maximized those opportunities to create new families.

Third, the more privilege a family has along lines of race, class, gender, and sexuality, the easier it will be for that family to maintain itself and gain respect from those around them. More often than not, social respect translates into policies that sustain privileged families and therefore help perpetuate the myth that only certain families are "good" and "healthy." Conversely, the less privilege a particular group of people has, the more difficult it is to maintain their families, precisely because those with privilege give them little respect and little support through social policies. We continue to see how privilege and oppression shape families repeatedly throughout history when we look at the formation of African-American families, single-headed families, divorced families, blended families, and now lesbian and gay families.

Ultimately every type of American family has developed out of a particular social, cultural, political, economic, and historical context. Unfortunately, people with race, class, gender, and/or sexual privilege fail to recognize this context, pathologize the diversity of families, and do not acknowledge the necessity for policies that would truly support the needs of diverse families. My research on lesbians' decision-making processes supports the reality that until we recognize that families develop out of the contexts in which they exist, and that people—regardless of their race, class, gender, or sexual statuses—seek whatever opportunities they can to make choices about their families, we will continue to value a monolithic family form that is virtually extinct, that was never perfect, and that itself arose out of a particular historical moment that no longer exists.

Despite profound changes in recent years, and regardless of evidence to the contrary, we still today often hear from mainstream media, politicians, and even some social scientists that lesbians and gays are moving us away from "traditional family values" and creating immoral and troubled families that cause all sorts of societal problems (Popenoe, 1992). This type of thinking ignores the historical reasons why lesbian families have developed at this particular time and the ways in which lesbians have seized the opportunities provided by this historical moment. Change takes place at a particular time for particular reasons. Lesbians even thirty years ago could not have made the mothering decisions they do today. Social, political, economic, and cultural conditions have coalesced at this historical moment to create a social environment in which lesbians—particularly those privileged by race and class—can choose how to create new families. Forces that shape every aspect of our lives, forces organized along lines of race, class, gender, and sexuality, have offered lesbians varying types of opportunities to choose the members of their families. It is the vision lesbians create out of social and cultural opportunities that is partially responsible for how American families are currently changing. More broadly speaking, it is the interactions between people and their surroundings—and in this case, between lesbians and the larger social and cultural spaces within which they and their families are situated—that shape and reshape, define and redefine, motherhood and families today.

Recruitment Questionnaire

If you are willing to participate in a group interview for my study on lesbian's decisions to remain childfree or to mother, please answer the following questions:

Name:

Age:

Telephone # and/or email address:

City/Town of Residence:

Are you employed? yes _____ no _____

If you are employed, what is your occupation/job?

What is your highest level of education (e.g., high school, GED, Associates Degree, BA, MA)?

What is your racial background (e.g., African American, Latina, White/Caucasian, etc.)?

Do you have any children, are you or your partner pregnant, or are you or your partner in the process of adopting a child?

yes (please explain) _____

no _____

If you have children, are they from a previous heterosexual relationship or did you have/adopt them as a lesbian?

If you do not have any children, do you plan on having children in the future?

What days/times are you available to participate in a two- to three-hour group interview (e.g., evenings, weekends, etc.)?

Interview Guide for Lesbian Mothers

I'd like to ask you some questions about your personal beliefs, your work experiences, your ties to different communities and family members, and your personal relationships. The questions I am asking serve as a guide, so please feel free to elaborate on any of the questions and to ask your own questions.

1. Let's start out by discussing how you got to be mothers. What events led up to your decision to be a parent?

2. Tell me about your definitions of *mother*. What words come to mind when you think about *mother* (e.g., biological, power, social, burdened, etc.). Did how your definitions of *mother* affect your decision to become a mother yourself?

3. What about your families of origin? What do you think their definitions of *mother* are? Do/did your parents have ideas of what "proper" mothers are like? Did your families' definitions of *mother* affect your decision to become a mother yourself?

4. What about any larger communities you belong to (racial, class, religious, lesbian, gay, queer)? What do you think their definitions of *mother* are? Do/did people in those communities have ideas of what "proper" mothers should be like? Did your communities' definitions of *mother* affect your decision to become a mother yourself?

5. Did having a partner or not having a partner affect your decision to become a parent?

6. Do any of you have partners of different racial-ethnic, class, or other backgrounds? If so, has that difference affected your decision to parent? For those with partners of similar backgrounds, have the similarities affected your decisions?

7. Has your employment situation (i.e., having a job, not having a job, future work aspirations) affected your decisions to become parents?

8. What has your experience been with the medical community, if any?

9. Did the anticipated need to work with the medical community affect your decision to parent?

10. What has been your experience with the legal and social work community, if any?

11. Did the anticipated need to work with the legal and social work community affect your decision to parent?

12. In choosing alternative insemination, did the choice between known and unknown donors affect your decision to parent?

13. In choosing adoption, did the potential of adopting a special-needs child or a child of a different racial-ethnic background from yourself affect your decision to parent?

14. Do you feel integrated into a larger lesbian or gay or queer community? Has your integration or lack of integration affected your decision to mother?

15. What lesbian- or gay-centered resources (e.g., support groups, other lesbian parents, etc.) were available to you that made your decision to parent easier or harder?

16. What other resources (e.g., medical personnel, social workers, family members, etc.) were available to you that made your decision to parent easier or harder?

17. What resources have not been available to you and have made this decision more difficult?

18. Have you come out to your family of origin? Has your coming out or staying closeted influenced your decision to parent?

19. Does your family of origin know that you are planning on having children? If so, what has been their reaction? Has that reaction affected your decision to become a mother?

20. By lesbians' becoming parents, do you think that you are changing the nature of motherhood or trying to fit in to some heterosexual definition of motherhood? Did you think about this question before becoming a mother? If so, did it influence your decision to mother?

21. Did financial resources or constraints play a part in making the decision to parent? If so, how?

22. Has the HIV/AIDS epidemic affected your decision to mother in any way (e.g., wanting to bring children into a dying gay community, affected donor choices, affected choices about adopting children with HIV/AIDS, etc.)?

23. What have been some of the challenges you have faced in making the decision to parent?

24. Has your decision to parent been influenced by your own personal identity as a lesbian, as a woman, as having a career, or as belonging to a particular racial-ethnic or economic class? If so, how?

25. Have you felt any societal pressure to mother or to be childfree? If so, how has that affected your decision to parent?

26. Did you ever think that by having children, you would be forced to come out in more public situations? If so, did that affect your decision to mother?

27. Do you have anything you would like to add about how you arrived at the decision to mother or about how other lesbians might arrive at the decision to mother?

28. Do you think we've left anything out of this discussion that we should discuss?

29. Do you have any questions you would like to ask of me?

Interview Guide for Childfree Lesbians

I'd like to ask you some questions about your personal beliefs, your work experiences, your ties to different communities and family members, and your personal relationships. The questions I am asking serve as a guide, so please feel free to elaborate on any of the questions and to ask your own questions.

1. The research I am doing looks at how some lesbians decide to have children and other lesbians decide not to have children. Before we get started, I want to ask your opinion about the terms I am using. I have been referring to lesbians with children as *lesbian mothers* and lesbians without children as *childfree* lesbians. Do you think these are appropriate terms, or are there more appropriate terms to use?

2. What events led up to your decision to be childfree? Did you make a conscious decision to remain childfree, or has it just turned out that way?

3. Tell me about your definitions of *mother*. What words come to mind when you think about *mother* (e.g., biological, power, social, burdened, etc.). Did your definitions of *mother* affect your decision to be childfree?

4. What about your families of origin? What do you think their definitions of *mother* are? Do/did your parents have ideas of what "proper" mothers are like? Did your families' definitions of *mother* affect your decision to be childfree?

5. Do you belong to any larger communities (racial, class, religious, lesbian, gay, queer)? If so, what do you think their definitions of *mother* are? Do/did people in those communities have ideas of what "proper" moth-

ers should be like? Did your communities' definitions of *mother* affect your decision to be childfree?

6. Do any of you have partners of different racial-ethnic, class, or other backgrounds? If so, has that difference affected your decision to be child-free? For those with partners of similar backgrounds, have the similarities affected your decisions?

7. Did having a partner or not having a partner affect your decision to be childfree?

8. Has your employment situation (i.e., having a job, not having a job, future work aspirations) affected your decisions to be childfree?

9. What has your experience been with the medical community, if any?

10. Did the anticipated need to work with the medical community affect your decision to be childfree?

11. What has been your experience with the legal and social work community, if any?

12. Did the anticipated need to work with the legal and social work community affect your decision to be childfree?

13. Do you feel integrated into a larger lesbian or gay or queer community? Has your integration or lack of integration affected your decision to be childfree?

14. What lesbian- or gay-centered resources (e.g., support groups, other lesbian parents, etc.) were available to you that made your decision to be childfree easier or harder?

15. What other resources (e.g., medical personnel, social workers, family members, etc.) were available to you that made your decision to be child-free easier or harder?

16. What resources have not been available to you and have made this decision more difficult?

17. Have you come out to your family of origin? Has your coming out or staying closeted influenced your decision to remain childfree?

18. Does your family of origin know that you are planning on not having children? If so, what has been their reaction? Has that reaction affected your decision to remain childfree?

19. What have been some of the challenges you have faced in making the decision to remain childfree?

20. Did financial resources or constraints play a part in making the decision to remain childfree? If so, how?

21. Has your decision to remain childfree been influenced by your own personal identity as a lesbian, as a woman, as having a career, or as belonging to a particular racial-ethnic or economic class? If so, how?

22. Have you felt any societal pressure to mother or to remain childfree? If so, how has that affected your decision to be childfree?

23. Do you think that lesbians who are becoming mothers are changing the nature of motherhood in any way or are they trying to fit in to a heterosexual definition of motherhood? Did you think about this question before deciding to be childfree?

24. Has the HIV/AIDS epidemic community affected your decision to remain childfree? (e.g., not wanting to bring children into a dying gay community, affected donor choices, affected choices about adopting children with HIV/AIDS, etc.).

25. Did you ever think that by having children, you would be forced to come out in more public situations? If so, did that affect your decision to remain childfree?

26. Do you have anything you would like to add about how you arrived at the decision to remain childfree or about how other lesbians might arrive at the decision to be childfree?

27. Do you think we've left anything out of this discussion that we should discuss?

28. Do you have any questions you would like to ask of me?

References

Allen, J. (1983). Motherhood: The Annihilation of Women. In J. Trebilcot (Ed.), *Mothering: Essays in Feminist Theory* (pp. 315–30). Totowa, NJ: Rowman and Allanheld.

Ameristat. (2003). *Traditional Families Account for Only 7 Percent of U.S. Households.* Population Reference Bureau. Available: www.prb.org/Ameristat Template.cfm?Section=MarriageandFamily&template=/ContentManagement/ContentDisplay.cfm&ContentID=8288 [1996, 1/05/06].

Andersen, M. L. (1993). Studying across Difference: Race, Class, and Gender in Qualitative Research. In J. H. Stanfield II and R. M. Dennis (Eds.), *Race and Ethnicity in Research Methods* (pp. 39–52). Newbury Park, CA: Sage.

Andersen, M. L. (2006). *Thinking about Women: Sociological Perspectives on Sex and Gender* (4th ed.). Boston: Allyn and Bacon.

Andrews, K. (1995). Ancient Affections: Gays, Lesbians, and Family Status. In K. Arnup (Ed.), *Lesbian Parenting: Living with Pride and Prejudice* (pp. 358–77). Charlottetown, Canada: Gynery Books.

Anzaldúa, G. (1999). *Borderlands / La Frontera: The New Mestiza.* San Francisco: Aunt Lute Book Company.

Arnup, K. (1995). Living in the Margins: Lesbian Families and the Law. In K. Arnup (Ed.), *Lesbian Parenting: Living with Pride and Prejudice* (pp. 378–98). Charlottetown, Canada: Gynery Books.

Baca Zinn, M. (1979). Field Research in Minority Communities: Ethical, Methodological, and Political Observations by an Insider. *Social Problems, 27*(2), 209–19.

Baca Zinn, M., and Dill, B. T. (1996). Theorizing Difference from Multiracial Feminism. *Feminist Studies, 22*(2), 321–31.

Baca Zinn, M., and Eitzen, D. S. (2008). *Diversity in Families* (8th ed.). Boston: Allyn and Bacon.

Barrett, J. E., and Roediger, D. (2005). How White People Became White. In P. S. Rothenberg (Ed.), *White Privilege: Essential Readings on the Otherside of Racism* (pp. 35–40). New York: Worth.

Bartlett, J. (1994). *Will You Be Mother? Women Who Choose to Say No.* London: Virago.

Bennett, M., and Battle, J. (2001). "We Can See Them, but We Can't Hear Them": LGBT Members of African American Families. In M. Bernstein and R. Reimann (Eds.), *Queer Families, Queer Politics: Challenging Culture and the State* (pp. 53–67). New York: Columbia University Press.

Bernstein, J., and Stephenson, L. (1995). Dykes, Donors and Dry Ice: Alternative Insemination. In K. Arnup (Ed.), *Lesbian Parenting: Living with Pride and Prejudice* (pp. 3–15). Charlottetown, Canada: Gynery Books.

Black, D., Gates, G., Sanders, S., and Taylor, L. (2000). Demographics of the Gay and Lesbian Population in the United States: Evidence from Available Systematic Data Sources. *Demography, 37*(2), 139–54.

Blank, R. (1998). Regulation of Donor Insemination. In K. Daniels and E. Haimes (Eds.), *Donor Insemination: International Social Science Perspectives* (pp. 131–50). New York: Cambridge University Press.

Blum, L., and Deussen, T. (1996). Negotiating Independent Motherhood: Working Class African American Women Talk about Marriage and Motherhood. *Gender and Society, 10*(2), 199–211.

Boggis, T. (2001). Affording Our Families: Class Issues in Family Formation. In M. Bernstein and R. Reimann (Eds.), *Queer Families, Queer Politics* (pp. 175–81). New York: Columbia University Press.

Bolte, A. (1998). Do Wedding Dresses Come in Lavender? The Prospects and Implications of Same-Sex Marriage. *Social Theory and Practice, 24*(1), 111–31.

Bonilla-Silva, E. (2003). *Racism without Racists: Color-Blind Racism and the Persistence of Racial Inequality in the United States.* New York: Rowman and Littlefield.

Burawoy, M. (Ed.). (1991). *Ethnography Unbound: Power and Resistance in the Modern Metropolis.* Berkeley: University of California Press.

Butler, J. (1993). Imitation and Gender Subordination. In H. Abelove, M. A. Barale, and D. Halperin (Eds.), *The Lesbian and Gay Studies Reader* (pp. 307–20). New York: Routledge.

Cabaj, R. P. (1998). History of Gay Acceptance and Relationships. In R. P. Cabaj and D. W. Purcell (Eds.), *On the Road to Same-Sex Marriage: A Supportive Guide to Psychological, Political, and Legal Issues* (pp. 1–28). San Francisco: Jossey-Bass.

Cain, M. (2001). *The Childless Revolution: What It Means to Be Childless Today.* New York: Perseus.

Chabot, J. (1998). Transition to Parenthood: Lesbian Couples' Experiences with Donor Insemination. Ph.D. diss., Michigan State University, East Lansing.

Cherlin, A. J. (2004). The Deinstitutionalization of American Marriage. *Journal of Marriage and Family, 66* (November), 848–61.

Clarke, C. (1983). The Failure to Transform: Homophobia in the Black Community. In B. Smith (Ed.), *Home Girls: A Black Feminist Anthology* (pp. 197–208). New York: Kitchen Table/Women of Color.

Collins, P. H. (1990). *Black Feminist Thought: Knowledge, Consciousness, and Empowerment.* Boston: Unwin Hyman.

Collins, P. H. (1997). The Meaning of Motherhood in Black Culture and Black Mother-Daughter Relationships. In M. B. Zinn, P. Hondagneu-Sotelo, and M. A. Messner (Eds.), *Through the Prism of Difference: Readings on Sex and Gender* (pp. 264–75). Boston: Allyn and Bacon.

Connell, R. W., Davis, M. D., and Dowsett, G. W. (1993). A Bastard of a Life: Homosexual Desire and Practice among Men in Working-Class Milieux. *Australian and New Zealand Journal of Sociology, 29*(1), 112–35.

Coontz, S. (2000). *The Way We Never Were: American Families and the Nostalgia Trap.* New York: Basic Books.

Crittenden, A. (2001). *The Price of Motherhood: Why the Most Important Job in the World Is Still the Least Valued.* New York: Henry Holt. and Co.

Davis, A. Y. (1998). Surrogates and Outcast Mothers: Racism and Reproductive Politics in the Nineties. In J. James (Ed.), *The Angela Y. Davis Reader* (pp. 210–21). Malden, MA: Blackwell.

D'Emilio, J. (1983). *Sexual Politics, Sexual Communities: The Making of a Homosexual Minority in the United States, 1940–1970.* Chicago: University of Chicago Press.

D'Emilio, J. (1993). Capitalism and Gay Identity. In W. B. Rubenstein (Ed.), *Lesbians, Gay Men, and the Law* (pp. 26–31). New York: New Press.

DiLapi, E. M. (1989). Lesbian Mothers and the Motherhood Hierarchy. In F. W. Bozett (Ed.), *Homosexuality and the Family* (pp. 101–21). New York: Hawthorne.

Dill, B. T. (1994). Fictive Kin, Paper Sons, and Compadrazgo: Women of Color and the Struggle for Family Survival. In M. Baca Zinn and B. T. Dill (Eds.), *Women of Color in U.S. Society* (pp. 149–69). Philadelphia: Temple University Press.

Dill, B. T., Baca Zinn, M. and Patton, S. (1998). Valuing Families Differently: Race, Poverty and Welfare Reform. *Sage Race Relations Abstracts, 23*(3), 4–30.

DuBois, W. E. B. (1903/1994). *Souls of Black Folks.* Mineola, NY: Dover.

Dunne, G. A. (2000). Opting into Motherhood: Lesbians Blurring the Boundaries and Transforming the Meaning of Parenthood and Kinship. *Gender and Society, 14*(1), 11–35.

Eichler, M. (1996). The Construction of Technologically-Mediated Families. *Journal of Comparative Family Studies, 27*(Summer), 281–308.

Eitzen, D. S., and Baca Zinn, M. (2006). *In Conflict and Order: Understanding Society* (11th ed.). Upper Saddle River, NJ: Pearson.

Epstein, S. (1994). A Queer Encounter: Sociology and the Study of Sexuality. *Sociological Theory, 12*(2), 188–202.

Escoffier, J. (1992). Generations and Paradigms: Mainstreams in Lesbian and Gay Studies. *Journal of Homosexuality, 24*(1/2), 7–26.

Espín, O. M. (1997). *Latina Realities: Essays on Healing, Migration, and Sexuality*. Boulder, CO: Westview.

Faderman, L. (1991). *Odd Girls and Twilight Lovers: A History of Lesbian Life in Twentieth-Century America*. New York: Penguin.

Faderman, L. (1997). Outside the Inside. In J. Wells (Ed.), *Lesbians Raising Sons* (pp. 62–64). New York: Alyson Books.

Faux, M. (1984). *Childless by Choice: Choosing Childlessness in the Eighties*. Garden City, NY: Anchor/Doubleday.

Firestone, S. (1970). *The Dialectic of Sex: The Case for Feminist Revolution*. New York: William Morrow.

Fish, E. (2005). The Road to Recognition: A Global Perspective on Gay Marriage. *Harvard International Law, 27*(2), 32–35.

Flaks, D. K., Ficher, I., Masterpasqua, F., and Joseph, G. (1995). Lesbians Choosing Motherhood: A Comparative Study of Lesbian and Heterosexual Parents and Their Children. *Developmental Psychology, 31*(1), 105–14.

Foley, N. (2005). Becoming Hispanic: Mexican Americans and Whiteness. In P. S. Rothenberg (Ed.), *White Privilege: Essential Readings on the Otherside of Racism* (pp. 55–65). New York: Worth.

Gerson, K. (1985). *Hard Choices: How Women Decide about Work, Career, and Motherhood*. Berkeley: University of California Press.

Gerson, K., and Jacobs, J. (2004). The Work-Home Crunch. *Contexts, 3*(4), 29–37.

Giminez, M. (1983). Feminism, Pronatalism, and Motherhood. In J. Trebilcot (Ed.), *Mothering: Essays in Feminist Theory* (pp. 287–314). Totowa, NJ: Rowman and Allanheld.

Giminez, M. (1991). The Mode of Reproduction in Transition: A Marxist-Feminist Analysis of the Effects of Reproductive Technologies. *Gender and Society, 5*(3), 334–50.

Gold, S. (1997). A White Guy among Vietnamese Women. In M. Baca Zinn, P. Hondagneu-Sotelo, and M. A. Messner (Eds.), *Through the Prism of Difference: Readings on Sex and Gender*. Boston: Allyn and Bacon.

Gomes, C. (2003). Partners as Parents: Challenges Faced by Gays Denied Marriage. *Humanist, 63*(6), 14–19.

Gorelick, S. (1991). Contradictions of Feminist Methodology. *Gender and Society, 5*(4), 459–77.

Greene, B. (1994). Ethnic-Minority Lesbians and Gay Men: Mental Health and Treatment Issues. *Journal of Consulting and Clinical Psychology, 62*(2), 243–51.

Greene, B. (1998). Family, Ethnic Identity, and Sexual Orientation: African-American Lesbians and Gay Men. In C. J. Patterson and A. R. D'Augelli (Eds.), *Lesbian, Gay, and Bisexual Identities in Families: Psychological Perspectives* (pp. 40–52). New York: Oxford University Press.

Grov, C., Bimbi, D. S., Nanín, J. E., and Parsons, J. T. (2006). Race, Ethnicity, Gender, and Generational Factors Associated with the Coming-out Process among Gay, Lesbian, and Bisexual Individuals. *Journal of Sex Research*, 43(1), 115–21.

Hartman, A. (1999). The Long Road to Equality: Lesbians and Social Policy. In J. Laird (Ed.), *Lesbians and Lesbian Families: Reflections on Theory and Practice* (pp. 91–120). New York: Columbia University Press.

Health Pages (1996–98). *Fertility Clinic Report*. Health Pages. Available: www.thehealthpages.com/fertility/al-ivf.htm [1999, April].

Hequembourg, A. L. (2007). *Lesbian Motherhood: Stories of Becoming*. New York: Harrington Park.

Hertz, R. (2006). *Single by Chance, Mothers by Choice: How Women are Choosing Parenthood without Marriage and Creating the New American Family*. New York: Oxford University Press.

Hochschild, A. R. (1989). *The Second Shift: Working Parents and the Revolution at Home*. New York: Viking.

hooks, b. (1984). *Feminist Theory from Margin to Center*. Boston: South End.

hooks, b. (1989). *Talking Back: Thinking Feminist, Thinking Black*. Boston: South End.

HRC. (2004a). *Marriage/Relationship Laws: State by State*. Human Rights Campaign (HRC). Available: www.hrc.org/Template.cfm?Section=Marriage&CONTENTID=20716&TEMPLATE=/TaggedPage/TaggedPageDisplay.cfm&TPLID=66 [2005, August 8, 2005].

HRC. (2004b). *Recent Developments in Massachusetts*. Human Rights Campaign (HRC). Available: www.hrc.org/Template.cfm?Section=Marriage&CONTENTID=21686&TEMPLATE=/ContentManagement/ContentDisplay.cfm [2005, August 8, 2005].

HRC. (2004c). *Connecticut Marriage/Relationship Recognition Law*. Human Rights Campaign (HRC). Available: www.hrc.org/Template.cfm?Section=Marriage&CONTENTID=22399&TEMPLATE=/ContentManagement/ContentDisplay.cfm [2005, August 8, 2005].

HRC. (2004d). *Answers to Questions About Marriage*, [webpage]. Human Rights Campaign. Available: www.hrc.org/Template.cfm?Section=GetInvolved1&Template=/ContentManagement/ContentDisplay.cfm&ContentID=17262 [2005, July 21].

HRC. (2007). *New Hampshire Legislation/Ballot Initiatives Affecting GLBT People*. Human Rights Campaign (HRC). Available: http://hrc.org/Template.cfm?Section=New_Hampshire&Template=/CustomSource/Law/StateDisplay.cfm&StateCode=NH&LawFlag=0&StatusInd=legcurrent [2007, May 23, 2007].

Ireland, M. S. (1993). *Reconceiving Women: Separating Motherhood from Female Identity*. New York: Guilford.

Jarrett, R. (1993). Focus Group Interviewing with Low-Income Minority Populations: A Research Experience. In D. L. Morgan (Ed.), *Successful Focus Groups: Advancing the State of the Art* (pp. 184–201). Newbury Park, CA: Sage.

Jarrett, R. (1994). Living Poor: Family Life among Single Parent, African-American Women. *Social Problems, 41*(1), 30–49.

Johnson, A. G. (1997). *The Forest and the Trees: Sociology as Life, Practice, and Promise.* Philadelphia: Temple University Press.

Katz, J. N. (1996). *The Invention of Heterosexuality.* New York: Plume.

Kendell, K. (1998). Lesbian Couples Creating Families. In R. P. Cabaj and D. W. Purcell (Eds.), *On the Road to Same-Sex Marriage: A Supportive Guide to Psychological, Political, and Legal Issues* (pp. 41–57). San Francisco: Jossey-Bass.

Kennamer, J. D., Hannold, J., Bradford, J., and Hendricks, M. (2000). Differences in Disclosure of Sexuality among African American and White Gay/Bisexual Men: Implications for HIV/AIDS Prevention. *AIDS Education and Prevention, 12*(6), 519–31.

Kennedy, E. L., and Davis, M. D. (1993). *Boots of Leather, Slippers of Gold: The History of a Lesbian Community.* New York: Routledge.

Lamphere, L., Zavella, P., Gonzales, F., and Evans, P. B. (1993). *Sunbelt Working Mothers: Reconciling Family and Factory.* Ithaca, NY: Cornell University Press.

Lasker, J. N. (1998). The Users of Donor Insemination. In K. Daniels and E. Haimes (Eds.), *Donor Insemination: International Social Science Perspectives* (pp. 7–32). New York: Cambridge University Press.

Lee, C. A. (1992). An Asian Lesbian's Struggle. In M. Silvera (Ed.), *Piece of My Heart: A Lesbian of Colour Anthology* (pp. 115–18). Toronto: Sister Vision.

Lemonick, M. D. (1997). The New Revolution in Making Babies. *Time, 150* (December 1), 40–46.

Lewin, E. (1993). *Lesbian Mothers: Accounts of Gender in American Culture.* Ithaca, NY: Cornell University Press.

Lewin, E. (1994). Negotiating Lesbian Motherhood: The Dialectics of Resistance and Accommodation. In E. N. Glenn, G. Chang, and L. R. Force (Eds.), *Mothering: Ideology, Experience, and Agency* (pp. 333–53). New York: Routledge.

Lewin, E. (1995a). On the Outside Looking In: The Politics of Lesbian Motherhood. In F. D. Ginsburg and R. Rapp (Eds.), *Conceiving the New World Order: The Global Politics of Reproduction* (pp. 103–21). Berkeley: University of California Press.

Lewin, E. (1995b). Writing Lesbian Ethnography. In R. Behar and D. A. Gordon (Eds.), *Women Writing Culture* (pp. 322–35). Berkeley: University of California Press.

Lewin, E. (1998). *Recognizing Ourselves*. New York: Columbia University Press.

Lewin, E. (2004). Does Marriage Have a Future? *Journal of Marriage and Family, 66* (November), 1000–1006.

Lipsitz, G. (2005). The Possessive Investment in Whiteness. In P. S. Rothenberg (Ed.), *White Privilege: Essential Readings on the Otherside of Racism* (pp. 67–90). New York: Worth.

Loiacano, D. K. (1989). Gay Identity Issues among Black Americans: Racism, Homophobia, and the Need for Validation. *Journal of Counseling and Development, 68*(September/October), 21–25.

Lorde, A. (1984). *Sister Outsider: Essays and Speeches by Audre Lorde*. New York: Crossing Press.

Luttrell, W. (2000). "Good Enough" Methods for Ethnographic Research. *Harvard Educational Review, 70*(4), 499–515.

Markovitz, D. L. (2000). *The Vermont Guide to Civil Unions*. Office of the Secretary of State. Available: www.sec.state.vt.us/pubs/civilunions.htm [2001, November 13].

Martin, A. (1993). *The Lesbian and Gay Parenting Handbook: Creating and Raising Our Families*. New York: HarperCollins .

Martinez, E. (2007). Seeing More Than Black and White. In M. L. Andersen and P. H. Collins (Eds.), *Race, Class, and Gender: An Anthology* (pp. 105–11). Belmont, CA: Thomson/Wadsworth.

Mays, V. M., Cochran, S. D., and Rhue, S. (1993). The Impact of Perceived Discrimination on the Intimate Relationships of Black Lesbians. *Journal of Homosexuality, 25*(4), 1–14.

McDaniel, S. A. (1996). Toward a Synthesis of Feminist and Demographic Perspectives on Fertility. *Sociological Quarterly, 37*(Winter), 83–104.

McMahon, M. (1995). *Engendering Motherhood: Identity and Self-Transformation in Women's Lives*. New York: Guilford.

Mintz, S., and Kellogg, S. (1988). *Domestic Revolutions: A Social History of American Family Life*. New York: Free Press.

Mohr, R. D. (1994). *A More Perfect Union: Why Straight America Must Stand up for Gay Rights*. Boston: Beacon.

Mooney-Somers, J., and Golombok, S. (2000). Children of Lesbian Mothers: From the 1970s to the new Millennium. *Sexual and Relationship Therapy*, May, 121–26.

Moraga, C. (1997). *Waiting in the Wings: Portrait of a Queer Motherhood*. Ithaca, NY: Firebrand Books.

Morales, E. S. (1990). Ethnic Minority Families and Minority Gays and Lesbians. In F. W. Bozett and M. B. Sussman (Eds.), *Homosexuality and Family Relations* (pp. 217–40). New York: Harrington Park.

Morell, C. (1993). Intentionally Childless Women: Another View of Women's Development. *Affilia, 8*(3), 300–316.

Morell, C. (1994). *Unwomanly Conduct: The Challenges of Intentional Childlessness.* New York: Routledge.

Morgan, D. L. (1997). *Focus Groups as Qualitative Research.* Thousand Oaks, CA: Sage.

Morgan, D. L., and Krueger, R. A. (1993). When to Use Focus Groups and Why. In D. L. Morgan (Ed.), *Successful Focus Groups: Advancing the State of the Art* (pp. 3–19). Newbury Park, CA: Sage.

Morningstar, B. (1999). Lesbian Parents: Understanding Developmental Pathways. In J. Laird (Ed.), *Lesbians and Lesbian Families: Reflections on Theory and Practice* (pp. 213–41). New York: Columbia University Press.

Moskovitz, E. (1996). In the Courts: Same-Sex Couples. *Hastings Center Report,* July–August, 47–48.

Murphy, J. S. (2001). Should Lesbians Count as Infertile Couples? Antilesbian Discrimination in Assisted Reproduction. In M. Bernstein and R. Reimann (Eds.), *Queer Families, Queer Politics* (pp. 182–200). New York: Columbia University Press.

Muzio, C. (1999). Lesbian Coparenting: On Being/Being with the Invisible (M)other. In J. Laird (Ed.), *Lesbians and Lesbian Families: Reflections on Theory and Practice* (pp. 197–211). New York: Columbia University Press.

Newman, K. S. (1988). *Falling from Grace.* New York: Free Press.

Novaes, S. B. (1998). The Medical Management of Donor Insemination. In K. Daniels and E. Haimes (Eds.), *Donor Insemination: International Social Science Perspectives* (pp. 105–30). New York: Cambridge University Press.

Ohnuki-Tierney, E. (1984). "Native" Anthropologists. *American Ethnologist,* 11(3), 584–85.

O'Sullivan, S. (1995). Dykes and Diapers: Why Children? *Deneuve Magazine,* 5(5) (October), 16.

Pies, C. (1988). *Considering Parenthood* (2nd ed.). Minneapolis: Spinsters Ink.

Polatnick, M. (1996). Diversity in Women's Liberation Ideology: How a Black and a White Group of the 1960s Viewed Motherhood. *Signs,* 21(3), 679–706.

Pollack, J. S. (1995). *Lesbian and Gay Families: Redefining Parenting in America.* New York: Franklin Watts.

Popenoe, D. (1992, December 26). The Controversial Truth: Two-Parent Families Are Better. *New York Times,* A21.

Popenoe, D. (1993). American Family Decline, 1960–1990: A Review and Appraisal. *Journal of Marriage and the Family,* 55(August), 527–55.

Purcell, D. W. (1998). Current Trends in Same-Sex Marriage. In R. P. Cabaj and D. W. Purcell (Eds.), *On the Road to Same-Sex Marriage: A Supportive Guide to Psychological, Political, and Legal Issues* (pp. 29–40). San Francisco: Jossey-Bass.

Rasi, R. A., and Rodriquez-Nogues, L. (Eds.). (1995). *Out in the Workplace.* Los Angeles: Alyson.

Reimann, R. (2001). Lesbian Mothers at Work. In M. Bernstein and R. Reimann (Eds.), *Queer Families, Queer Politics: Challenging Culture and the State* (pp. 254–71). New York: Columbia University Press.

Rich, A. (1976). *Of Woman Born: Motherhood as Experience and Institution.* New York: Norton.

Rich, A. (1993). Compulsory Heterosexuality and Lesbian Existence. In H. Abelove, M. A. Barale, and D. Halperin (Eds.), *The Lesbian and Gay Studies Reader* (pp. 227–54). New York: Routledge.

Robson, R. (1992). Mother: The Legal Domestication of Lesbian Existence. *Hypatia, 7*(4), 172–85.

Rothblum, E. D., and Brehony, K. A. (1993). *Boston Marriages: Romantic but Asexual Relationships among Contemporary Lesbians.* Amherst: University of Massachusetts Press.

Rothman, B. K. (1989). *Recreating Motherhood: Ideology and Technology in a Patriarchal Society.* New York: Norton.

Rubin, G. (1993). Thinking Sex: Notes for a Radical Theory of the Politics of Sexuality. In H. Abelove, M. A. Barale, and D. Halperin (Eds.), *The Lesbian and Gay Studies Reader* (pp. 3–44). New York: Routledge.

Rubin, L. (1992). *Worlds of Pain: Life in the Working-Class Family* (new paperback ed.). New York: Basic Books.

Rubin, L. (1994). *Families on the Fault Line: America's Working Class Speaks about the Family, the Economy, Race, and Ethnicity.* New York: HarperCollins.

Rust, P. (2006). The Impact of Multiple Marginalization. In E. Disch (Ed.), *Reconstructing Gender: A Multicultural Anthology* (pp. 285–92). New York: McGraw-Hill.

Rust, P. C. (1992). The Politics of Sexual Identity: Sexual Attraction and Behavior among Lesbian and Bisexual Women. *Social Problems, 39*(4), 366–86.

Sedgwick, E. K. (1993). Epistemology of the Closet. In H. Abelove, M. A. Barale, and D. Halperin (Eds.), *The Lesbian and Gay Studies Reader* (pp. 45–61). New York: Routledge.

Segura, D. A. (1994). Working at Motherhood: Chicana and Mexican Immigrant Mothers and Employment. In E. N. Glenn, G. Chang, and L. R. Force (Eds.), *Mothering: Ideology, Experience, and Agency* (pp. 211–33). New York: Routledge.

Segura, D. A., and Pierce, J. L. (1993). Chicana/o Family Structure and Gender Personality: Chodorow, Familism, and Psychoanalytic Sociology Revisited. *Signs, 19*(1), 62–91.

Silber, L. D. (1991). *Dykes with Tykes: Becoming a Lesbian Mother.* Ann Arbor: University of Michigan Press.

Silvera, M. (1995). Confronting the "I" in the Eye: Black Mothers, Black Daughters. In K. Arnup (Ed.), *Lesbian Parenting: Living with Pride and Prejudice* (pp. 311–20). Charlottetown, Canada: Gynery Books.

Smith, B.(1983). Introduction. In B. Smith (Ed.), *Home Girls: A Black Feminist Anthology* (pp. xix–lvi). New York: Kitchen Table/Women of Color.

Smith, B. (1998). *The Truth That Never Hurts: Writings on Race, Gender, and Freedom.* New Brunswick, NJ: Rutgers University Press.

Smith, R. (2007). "Mexicanness" in New York: Migrants Seek New Place in Old Racial Order. In M. L. Andersen and P. H. Collins (Eds.), *Race, Class, and Gender: An Anthology* (pp. 214–20). Belmont, CA: Thomson/Wadsworth.

Snowden, R., and Snowden, E. (1998). Families Created through Donor Insemination. In K. Daniels and E. Haimes (Eds.), *Donor Insemination: International Social Science Perspectives* (pp. 33–52). New York: Cambridge University Press.

Stacey, J. (1988). Can There Be a Feminist Ethnography? *Women's Studies International Forum, 11*(1), 21–27.

Stacey, J. (1996). *In the Name of the Family: Rethinking Family Values in the Postmodern Age.* Boston: Beacon.

Stacey, J. (1998). Gay and Lesbian Families: Queer Like Us. In M. A. Mason, A. Skolnick, and S. D. Sugarman (Eds.), *All Our Families: New Policies for a New Century* (pp. 117–43). New York: Oxford University Press.

Stacey, J., and Biblarz, T. J. (2001). (How) Does the Sexual Orientation of Parents Matter? *American Sociological Review, 66*(April), 159–83.

Stein, A., and Plummer, K. (1994). "I Can't Even Think Straight:" "Queer" Theory and the Missing Sexual Revolution in Sociology. *Sociological Theory, 12*(2), 178–87.

Steiner, L. M. (2006). *The Mommy Wars: Stay-at-Home and Career Moms Face off on Their Choices, Their Lives, Their Families.* New York: Random House.

Sullivan, M. (1996). Rozzie and Harriet? Gender and Family Patterns of Lesbian Coparents. *Gender and Society, 10*(6), 747–67.

Sullivan, M. (2004). *The Family of Woman: Lesbian Mothers, Their Children, and the Undoing of Gender.* Berkeley: University of California Press.

Taylor, H. F. (2006). Defining Race. In E. Higginbotham and M. L. Andersen (Eds.), *Race and Ethnicity in Society: The Changing Landscape* (pp. 47–54). Belmont, CA: Thomson/Wadsworth.

Thompson, J. M. (2002). *Mommy Queerest: Contemporary Rhetorics of Lesbian Maternal Identity.* Amherst: University of Massachusetts Press.

Thompson, L. (1992). Feminist Methodology for Family Studies. *Journal of Marriage and the Family,* February, 3–18.

Thorne, B. (1992). Feminism and the Family: Two Decades of Thought. In B. Thorne and M. Yalom (Eds.), *Rethinking the Family: Some Feminist Questions* (2nd ed., pp. 3–30). Boston: Northeastern University Press.

Tong, L. (1998). Comparing Mixed-Race and Same-Sex Marriage. In R. P. Cabaj and D. W. Purcell (Eds.), *On the Road to Same-Sex Marriage: A Supportive*

Guide to Psychological, Political, and Legal Issues (pp. 109–28). San Francisco: Jossey-Bass.

Veevers, J. E. (1980). *Childless by Choice.* Toronto: Butterworths.

Wald, J. (1997). Outlaw Mothers. *Hastings Women's Law Review, 8*(1), 169–93.

Weeks, J. (2003). *Sexuality* (2nd ed.). New York: Routledge.

Weston, K. (1991). *Families We Choose: Lesbians, Gays, Kinship.* New York: Columbia University Press.

Whitehead, B. D. (1993). Dan Quayle Was Right. *The Atlantic, 271*(4), 47–84.

Zavella, P. (1987). *Women's Work and Chicano Families: Cannery Workers of the Santa Clara Valley.* Ithaca, NY: Cornell University Press.

Index